The Words I Chose

The Words I Chose

a memoir of family and poetry

Wesley McNair

Carnegie Mellon University Press
Pittsburgh 2012

Design: James Berndt and Sara-Anne Lee

Library of Congress Control Number 2011943581
ISBN 978-0-88748-557-2
Printed and bound in the United States of America

10 9 8 7 6 5 4 3 2

for my family

Foreword

For help with this book about my beginnings as a poet I have many people to thank, including Patricia Burdick, head of Special Collections at Colby College, for providing relevant documents from my archive; my mother and my wife Diane for preserving some of those documents in the first place; my brother Paul and half-sister Patty for information about my father; Sylvia Cypher for technical support; David Scribner for copy-editing; and a group of readers of an early draft, including Diane, Ellen Cooney, George Core, Peter Harris, Robert Kimber, Patricia O'Donnell, and especially Bill Roorbach, for invaluable suggestions. Thanks also to David Godine, Publisher, for permission to reprint the poems cited in this memoir, all of which come from *Lovers of the Lost, New & Selected Poems*, except two ("The Future" 2, "Draw Me"), first published in *The Ghosts of You and Me*. Final thanks go to United States Artists for the USA fellowship in poetry that steeled my nerves for this project and helped to fund it.

The Words I Chose is as close to my actual experience as I can make it. Like other memoirists, I have occasionally written dialogue for scenes that happened long ago. Obviously, I can't vouch for the accuracy of those conversations, though in every case I have stayed true to the intent and feeling I recall from the actual exchange, and to the characters with the speaking parts.

This book has taught me how much I owe my family for the poetry I ended up writing, not only its content but its vision. Like all families, mine has given me both pleasure and pain. I am sorry for the trouble we have caused each other, my family and I, but I am grateful for it as well, since without it I would have been denied the life I have known as a poet.

Wesley McNair
Temple, Maine

Chapter 1

Wanted

"Wanted" was the word I chose
for him at age eight, drawing the face
of a bad guy with comic-book whiskers
then showing it to my mother. This was how,

after my father left us, I made her smile
at the same time I told her I missed him,
and how I managed to keep him close by
in that house of perpetual anger,

becoming his accuser and his devoted
accomplice. I learned by writing
to negotiate between what I had,
and that more distant thing I dreamed of.

—"How I Became a Poet"

At first glance, the large photograph from 1943 of my father and mother outside their apartment house in Springfield, Vermont, offers no clue that he will soon leave her. It is just months after the birth of my brother John, the last of their three children, and they are standing side by side with their arms around each other's waists, astonishingly young, he twenty-five and she twenty-two. Rediscovering the photo all these years after his abandonment, I notice for the first time a distance between the two of them, even as they hold each other. And just behind my father's scowl in the harsh sunlight—do I only imagine it?—he seems remote, as though he has things other than picture-taking on his mind. Meanwhile my mother, her long hair carefully braided in pigtails, smiles for the camera as the proud wife.

My father, Wilbur Frank McNair, and my mother, Eileen Ruth Willard, met in a church during the summer of 1938 in Columbia, Missouri. Twenty years old then, he had just finished his freshman year at the University of Illinois and was working his way through college by selling subscriptions to *Better Homes and Gardens* magazine. She was seventeen, a high school graduate who had enrolled at the University of Missouri, in Columbia. During a phone call my mother of today tells me that my father went to the church because he could sell more magazines by attending church services than going door-to-door. There, he introduced himself to her and the female cousin she was staying with. Only three months later, on September 6, after another meeting and several letters back and forth from Columbia to Urbana, my parents got married.

"Are you sure you saw him only twice beforehand?" I ask my mother, thinking I must have misheard. "Two times," she says again, growing annoyed. "Why are you asking questions about him all of a sudden?" At age eighty-five, though she is the widow of another man, my stepfather, with whom she spent nearly all of her married life, my father's desertion is still a fresh wound. I don't mention the photograph I've rediscovered. Nor do I say that I'm thinking about starting a memoir, which has made me curious about her early life and his. I settle for the partial and more acceptable truth that I'm trying to find out more about our family's history. The approach works, though when I suggest she must have loved him a great deal to have married him so quickly, she goes silent.

The 1943 photo makes clear why the two of them were drawn to each other. Even after the birth of three children, my mother is an attractive woman with a youthful figure. For his part, my father is tall and movie-idol handsome. Still, it was not only his good looks that made my mother leap into marriage after a short courtship. She wanted to escape once and for all the hardscrabble and hard-luck life of her family from the Missouri Ozarks. According to my Uncle Truman, who recalled his sister of seventeen at a recent Willard family reunion, she "couldn't wait to get rid of the name of Willard."

My mother's upbringing was a miserable one that included extreme poverty and a migration from Missouri to Texas and back again during the Dust Bowl period. As the oldest of five children born to Daisy and Truston Willard, she scarcely had a childhood at all. In a questionnaire she once filled out for a grandchild's school project on family history, she described her labor this way:

> I could cut a freshly butchered chicken into twelve pieces when I was ten years old. At the time I looked after two babies. I changed and washed a lot of diapers. I also washed all the family clothes, heating up water drawn from the well (we had no running water or electricity) and scrubbing the clothes on a washboard outside.

Left in charge when my grandparents went to work in the cotton fields, my mother prepared all the meals and tended to the younger children. If her siblings did anything wrong on her watch, she once told me, she was the one who got the whipping. Most of the family whippings were administered by my grandmother, a woman my Uncle Truman says liked settling the score. Her reprisals took the form of sarcasm, hard slaps, and switches she made her children cut themselves. In the questionnaire, my mother hints at my grandmother's harsh discipline in passages that mix respect with a still-lingering resentment. She relates that Daisy permitted "no sassing" from her children, adding: "You couldn't even ask 'What's for lunch?'" Comparing the personalities of her father and mother in another passage, she calls Truston "quiet and kind" and Daisy, by contrast, "bossy and curt," a parent who "laid down the law all the time."

The one alternative to the dawn-to-dusk drudgery of life in the Ozarks was school, and though the local schoolhouse had only one teacher in a room that included eight grades, it provided my mother with a temporary escape. "I loved school," she reports. After she graduated from eighth grade, she twice convinced her parents to send her away to the homes of relatives so she could attend high school, ending up the second time with her aunt and uncle in Columbia, where she got her high school diploma. At the family home in Fowler, there were no books except two: the Bible and Daniel Defoe's *Robinson Crusoe*. She writes that as a young girl she read *Robinson Crusoe* "over and over by kerosene lamps." It is not hard to imagine the book's formative influence on her. Defoe's story of a hero who was trapped on an island and put aside his dreams of freedom while he busied himself with the hard work of survival is not so far removed from my mother's own story in the backwoods of the Ozarks. Longing for a life apart from the chores and isolation of rural Missouri, she no doubt found a kindred spirit in Crusoe. As she grew older, she perhaps longed for a companion who might share her developing interior life as well. In my father, the college man three years her senior, she found this companion, different from Crusoe's Friday in that he spoke her language. His letters from Illinois no doubt showed an interest in ideas and education that mirrored hers. When he proposed by letter that they marry and live together in Columbia while they both obtained their college degrees there, it must have seemed to her like a dream come true.

My father, who grew up on a farm more prosperous than my mother's, brought his own dreams to his marriage, or so it seems to me reading between the lines of what my brother Paul, who once lived with him, has told me about my father's early life. Whereas my mother had to contend with my strict and unsympathetic grandmother, he had to deal with my grandfather, Frank, who often held him up for ridicule. Unlike his two brothers, my father preferred ideas and books to farm work, and my grandfather nicknamed him "Speed" for his habit of walking home from school as slowly as possible to avoid joining his brothers with the chores. Probably my grandfather's sarcasm was inspired in part by how close his son was to my grandmother Verna. Wilbur was her favorite child, and she encouraged him to believe he was special and destined for great things.

My mother once told me about the gift Frank gave Verna for Christmas: a brand-new broom. My grandmother woke up in the morning to find it leaning against her side of the bed. This story suggests how little he valued or even knew her beyond her capacities as a housewife. Through her relationship with my father, she was no doubt able to express the feelings Frank would have considered a weakness in her, and to rebel against his ungenerous authority. When my father met my mother in the summer of 1938, he was straight off the farm and about as provincial as she was. But given Verna's influence, he had little sense of his limitations. He thought of himself as an intellectual and a writer on his way to the life for which her high opinion had prepared him.

The clues that my father had an outsized notion of his own powers were there from the start, my mother says, though she didn't see them at the time. Despite his pretentions as a writer, she got much better grades than he did in the composition course they took together at the University of Missouri. Seeing her success, he asked her to help him with his papers, and finally, to write them for him. Because my mother was in love and pleased by my father's praise of her work, she overlooked his inflated idea of his writing skills. Nor did she blame him at the end of the semester when his unrealistic plan of completing college together fell apart for lack of funds. Though being forced to leave college after one term upset her, it no doubt upset him as well, and their marriage seemed to both of them worth the sacrifice.

After my mother got pregnant in the late winter and they moved to Clarksburg, Missouri, there were more bad signs about my father, she says, though she continued to believe in him. To support her, he went back to selling magazines, promising large sales from his new territories, and each week while he was away, she stayed by herself in a room they rented from a man who lived downstairs and had, she feared, predatory motives. Waiting for my father to make good on his promises, she went without food sometimes for a day or more. In desperation, she began to ask the man for vegetables from his garden, fearing each time that she risked unwelcome advances. Yet each week my father returned without enough money for groceries, only occasionally paying the rent. Somehow she survived both her hunger and the landlord until she had carried my brother Paul to term. Once he was born, my father quit his job on the magazine crew and asked his parents to take him in, informing them about his marriage and his newborn son for the first time.

Of course, the results of this belated information were catastrophic for my father. Throughout the period the three of them stayed at the farmhouse in Dahlgren, my grandmother was inconsolable, upset that he had ruined his chance for an education by what he had done, and dashing her high expectations for him in the bargain. Though my mother in old age has often forgotten the particulars of long-ago events, she remembers my grandparents' behavior during the Dahlgren stay vividly. "She cried just about every day," my mother says, "and she cried about everything." Once Verna found her son wearing the sport coat he had purchased for his trips as a magazine salesman and noticed a red thread "you could hardly see" running through its fabric. In anguish because my father had chosen a jacket so "loud," she burst into tears. As for my grandfather, he found in my father's return to the farmhouse a source of personal vindication. Frank had never understood why my father wanted to leave the farm for a college degree in the first place. In his view, the predicament his son had gotten himself into showed what the world had in store for people with big ideas. His new nickname for his son was "college boy," and he employed it liberally, addressing not only my father but also Verna, who had supported the foolishness of sending him off to college in the first place. His mockery inspired still more tears.

To escape the family conflict and Verna's crying, my mother periodically left the house and closed herself in the privy. But she could not escape her mother-in-law's criticism, which was continuous and based on rules as strict and old-fashioned as my grandfather's were. Infants were supposed to wear black socks, Verna told her when she observed my brother wearing white ones. She recoiled when my mother wanted to give him store-bought baby food. In fact, nothing my mother did was right. "I spent most of my day sewing clothes for him and nursing," my mother recalls, "putting off my own needs until he went to sleep. Her response was to criticize me for washing my hair at nighttime, which according to her, women were not supposed to do."

During the Dahlgren visit, while his father and brothers did farm chores, my father occupied himself with assuaging his mother's daily grief. Perhaps he also wrote verses of poetry from time to time, trying them out on my mother. He often told her of his plan to make money by writing poetry for greeting cards. "Nothing ever came of it," she says tersely. Nothing came of his attempt to start a second newspaper in Dahlgren, either, though the two of them devoted a great deal of energy to the project. Out for a walk one night in town, my father saw a light on at the local printshop and went in to find a large press, perfect for printing a newspaper. He used his powers of persuasion to convince the printshop's owner how much money a newspaper could make. On my father's promise of sharing the profits, the man agreed to let him use the press after hours, even offering my parents the vacant room above the shop and meals with his family during the start-up period.

It is pleasant to think about the two of them as they left the oppression of Frank and Verna's house, buoyed by the prospect of making a living through their writing. My mother, having established herself as a

writer in her college composition class, became a reporter whenever
she was not busy with her new child, and my father began a campaign to
sell ads. "He told me, 'We're going to clean up with this,'" my mother
says. But it is hard to see how my father's scheme could have worked. He
had, after all, only a staff of two to research and write the newspaper's
articles, hand-set type on the old press, print and circulate the paper, and
sell the advertising. It was the advertising, in any case, that proved to be
the crucial obstacle. Most of the merchants who might be interested in
buying the ads were located in the nearby town of Mount Vernon; yet my
father, lacking a car, had no way to get there. Only a few weeks after he
had hatched his plan for a newspaper in Dahlgren, the venture failed, and
he was looking for employment elsewhere.

The place he and his young family finally landed was Groveton, New
Hampshire, where his first cousin was a minister. In Groveton, he wrote
my father, the paper mill was hiring workers. So my father moved his
family east, finding temporary quarters at his cousin's parsonage and a
job at the Groveton mill. A few months later, he migrated to employment
that was more to his liking several miles south in Newport, at the branch
office of the *Claremont Daily Eagle*. By then it was 1941, the year the
United States entered World War II, and he began to worry about being
drafted into the service. Advised that he could escape the draft by obtain-
ing employment at a company that manufactured military supplies, he left
the newspaper office not long after he started there, taking a job at the
Jones and Lamson machine shop in Springfield, Vermont. In Southview,
a housing project for J & L workers within walking distance of the shop,
he rented an apartment for his family. Meanwhile, my mother continued
to bear children. By the time she was twenty-one she had given birth
to three: I was born in 1941, and my brother John came along twelve
months afterward. In less than four years, she had turned from a college
girl into the woman we three knew as "Mama." This was the name she
had called her own mother in the Ozarks and now called herself, writ-
ing "Mama and Daddy" in my photo album beneath the large photograph
showing her and my father with their arms around each other's waists.

My photo album was not the only one my mother put together. She
made albums for my brothers during their growing-up years, too, care-
fully and lovingly inking in white captions on each black page. When we

13

were all old enough, she gave us our albums, considerable gifts. Mine begins with photos of me alone, mixed with snapshots of me and Paul. In the latter pictures the two of us are napping together, or he is reading me a magazine, or—in a photo that must have been difficult for my mother to set up—he is feeding me a marshmallow at a picnic directly from a stick. "Getting a bite of marshmallow," says the caption. The photo beside it shows me with a marshmallow in my hand, above the caption, "Picnics make me happy." On the following page Paul and I are all dressed up and standing at either end of a toy wagon occupied by our new brother John. Under this snapshot my mother has written, "We are all happy."

Johnny's birth gave my mother new storylines for the album. Two pages after the photo of him in the wagon, we sit one-two-three, youngest to oldest, up the porch steps of our apartment building in Southview. "Steps," reads the caption. Standing together in the yard, we become "The Three Musketeers." Later, we are pictured in a group of kids from the neighborhood, all named individually and labeled collectively as "The Gang." More than a gathering of photographs, the album presents the legend of a family my mother has created in pictures and words, a family whose children are the main characters. The chapter titles of this narrative are the years she has printed at the tops of pages, beginning with the year of my birth. The narrative's theme is happiness and togetherness—even when my father is no longer shown. I still remember sorely missing my father during the middle 1940s, when he was seldom at home and finally vanished from our family. But in the snapshots my mother took of me in that period, I find no clue of the pain I felt, so frequent is my smile. Though the three albums my mother gave us have different colors, their covers bear the identical image of a beleaguered Uncle Sam who steers a ship while around him cannons go off and planes fly. This image refers to the conflict between the United States and the Axis powers during World War II, but for me, it also suggests my mother's struggle as my father gradually extricated himself from our family. The three albums she made were crucial to her in that struggle, and the only novels she ever wrote. Returning to them with white ink and snapshots throughout the 1940s and beyond, she denied the emotional and economic wreckage my father left behind with her alternative story of family contentment.

My father's eventual success in the workplace led to his failure as
a husband and a father. After a stint at the machine shop in Springfield,
Vermont, he was asked to help establish a union there, and he found that
he liked union organizing. It did not require physical labor or mechani-
cal work, neither of which he cared for, and he enjoyed taking charge
of meetings with fellow workers and distributing broadsides he wrote
about union activities. Even my mother admits he was good at his new
job, and my brother Paul, who has learned the details of the early union
work, agrees. No doubt my father found the left-wing politics of union-
izing comfortably at odds with his father's staid Republicanism. In fact, as
his success grew and he was tapped for labor activities at other factories
in Vermont and greater New England, he created an identity that was
opposed to his father's values in other ways. Where my grandfather Frank
kept long and regular hours as a farmer ("he ruined me for nine-to-five
work," my father told my mother), my father improvised his working
hours and activities, often setting up meetings outside of the plant when
the day was done. Where Frank was a devout teetotaler and non-smoker,
my father regularly held forth in bars, drinking heavily and puffing on
cigarettes as he laid strategy about disrupting the very status quo my
grandfather's values and politics endorsed. Frank would surely have been
horrified if he knew that his son often advocated Communism at his union
meetings and was a card-carrying Communist.

Becoming the Un-Frank in his personal and work life and gaining a
reputation for his union efforts, my father fell into occasional relation-
ships with the female assistants who not only helped him with his union
activities but, because he had neither a car nor a license to drive, chauf-
feured him from place to place. Eventually, he was noticed by a fellow
organizer named Sylvia Wachs.

In most respects Sylvia was the Un-Ruth. A college-educated daugh-
ter of strictly moral missionaries, she was involved in her own rebellion
against parental authority and prided herself on being an unconventional
woman—disdainful of housekeeping, determined to compete with men
as an equal, and free in love, whether the man was married or not. What
was more, she had her own car. Soon she was at my father's side in his
late-night sessions, drinking, smoking, and talking ideas with him and
the other men. Against Sylvia, my mother never really had a chance. By

the time my father fell in love with his new companion, my mother had grown skeptical of his promises and self-aggrandizing stories. Sylvia countered that skepticism with a belief as strong as my mother's once was. For Sylvia, he was not "all talk," as my mother had begun to believe, but a fellow intellectual. Rather than nag him about the family bills that continued to mount because he was spending all his money on the road, Sylvia both applauded his achievements in his new work, and shared in them.

There is a photo in my album that shows a front view of my father in a rowboat lifting his oars and turning his head to one side. The snapshot underscores why the two women were attracted to him. He is tall, thin and handsome in his profile, with dark hair swept back from a widow's peak like those of movie posters in the 1940s. Whenever I got my photograph album out after my father left, it was this snapshot, together with the large photo of my parents side-by-side in Southview, that I went back to again and again. I was drawn not only to my father but to myself, just visible below him as I sat with my brother Paul in the boat, looking off at the water. Examing the snapshot today, I am reminded of Thomas Hardy's poem, "The Self-Unseeing," in which a narrator returns to a moment in his past when he was caught up in the pleasure of events and oblivious of the changes time would bring.

> Childlike, I danced in a dream;
> Blessings emblazoned that day
> Everything glowed with a gleam;
> Yet we were looking away.

Like my brother and me, my mother is also "looking away," even as she aims the camera at my father and tries to fit us all into the vignette that she has titled "Daddy Rowing." A few pages later she has aimed her camera at a guest of the family, who also rows a boat carrying my brothers and me: Sylvia Wachs herself.

Under the heading "Christmas, 1948" in the album, on a page that is black except for three snapshots, the family consists only of my mother, who took the pictures, and the three children wearing identical bathrobes who pose for her. In two of the photos, I am reaching under the small Christmas tree mounted on a table, as if to take out one of the few gifts assembled there, and my brothers are seated on the floor, both pretending to unwrap the presents in their laps. In the third picture we are on the floor together in our usual group pose, from oldest to youngest, each holding a present and smiling as if the most joyful thing for children on Christmas were to sit and hold unwrapped gifts.

The actual event that occasioned these photographs was not joyful at all, but heartbreaking. After an absence of months, my father promised from the road that he would be with us all on Christmas Eve, the night when the snapshots were taken, but he never showed up. My mother had sewn the bathrobes we wore for the event, and three of the unwrapped packages in the photo contain slippers she made, embroidering bunnies on them. Obviously, she had worked hard to set the stage for my father's reunion with his family. When it was bedtime and she saw the reunion would not happen, she took these pictures, attempting to transform heartbreak into continuity and enjoyment. Examining them closely, I discover a familiar photograph within one of the photographs: a portrait of her mother on a shelf near the Christmas tree.

The image of my grandmother Daisy in that portrait was at the edge of my awareness all through my childhood. I did not know then how much she had to do with my mother's zeal as a disciplinarian. Like my grandmother, my mother believed in the motto, "Spare the rod and spoil the child," and, despite her mixed feelings about her mother's disciplinary methods, as expressed in the school questionnaire she filled out years later, she kept a switch that she used regularly on me and my brothers. One morning when I was perhaps four, after my father had returned from the road to spend the night, I remember going into my parents' bedroom with Johnny so we could show him the marks from my mother's switch on our hands, which we had put behind us to protect ourselves during a whipping.

Johnny and I turned to my father because he was the lenient one of the two. When company came, it was he who bragged about us, trotting us out to recite our numbers or to perform a song we had learned by heart. In all the time he lived with us, he didn't speak a harsh word to me or my brothers, and this, I remember, made my mother worry that he was spoiling us. She once persuaded him to take me over his knee for a spanking, but he didn't have the heart for it and stopped shortly after he began. He was more comfortable taking our side when she threatened punishment. That, of course, upset her all the more. So she administered most of her punishments when he was away.

As the length of my father's absences grew, my mother's anger toward him deepened. Staying up late at night to do the seamstress work that supported us, she must have mulled her fate as an overworked child and surrogate parent who was now, just a few years later, stuck in the role of a parent once again. The difference was, of course, that now, she had to go it alone with no husband to help her, and because her mother had warned all her offspring not to "come running back" to the homestead in the Ozarks once they had left home, she was stuck in the still unfamiliar culture of New England with no way out. For us kids, she became a terrifying figure in this period. The smallest transgression could touch off her rage. Misinterpret her instructions or object to them, and we might land among shoes on the floor of a locked closet, kept there for hours. Forget to flush the toilet, and she held our heads in it while she flushed the toilet for us. "I work my fingers to the bone, and this is how you treat me?" she would ask.

Whippings were constant, the earliest ones dispensed with a switch, the later and worse ones with yardsticks my mother replaced as she broke them. Sometimes she spanked me for trying to do good things that somehow went bad. One afternoon I gave Johnny's doll and mine a bath, scrubbing them even harder when gray began to show through their pink cheeks. When my mother, out on an errand, came through the front door, Johnny ran to her in tears. "Come and see what Wesley did to my doll," he said. My mother came with a yardstick in her hand. Another day, stopping on my way to school to protect a frog from the attacks of a large dog, I was an hour late, and my first-grade teacher complained to her. "But I was trying to help the frog," I cried as she bent me over a chair in our living room. Such protests often made her whippings more severe. Once the beatings started, all she wanted to hear was the word no. "Is this what you wanted?" she would ask, swinging her yardstick, or "Are you ever going to do that again?" Holding my bare legs, I would get up and run until she forced me over another chair, and then another. There was no way now, of course, to appeal to my father. Yet he was always present, for his betrayal fueled my mother's rage, and as she spanked me in sessions that seemed never to end, I felt I was somehow to blame for all that had gone wrong in our house.

My mother's emotional instability and maltreatment were exacerbated by long stretches of work in the years after my father left. When she wasn't sewing clothes for my siblings and me, she was sewing for a growing list of customers, and on Saturdays, with a pair of electric clippers she bought for the purpose, she cut the hair of boys in the neighborhood, saving our haircuts for last. It was hard not to jump as the overheated clippers grazed our ears. "Stop squirming," she would say with a hard slap. "Keep up that whining and I'll give you something to whine about." We felt safer when my mother worked at her sewing machine, for though she abandoned us for hours as she sewed, we were nonetheless spared her punishments. Eventually, however, her day-and-night bouts of sewing led to her hospitalization for exhaustion.

When she returned home and the neighbors who had housed Paul, Johnny and me deposited us, we had two reasons to obey and please my mother, not only to avoid punishment, but to make her less vulnerable to the emotional stress that had dispersed the family. In *Gulliver's Travels*, Jonathan Swift writes about Brobignagia, the land of the giants, where his hero meets up with an unpredictable, moody girl who is so much bigger than he is that she can hold him in her hand. Frightened she may toss him away at any moment, Gulliver must use all his wit to divert her. Gulliver's situation with the giant girl reminds me of my childhood, when my psychological security depended on the skills of balancing my mother's moods.

Tempestuous as my childhood was, there were occasional good days, when my mother seemed unburdened by her troubles. On some of the best of them she read me the stories of a fictional black boy named Little Brown Koko that were serialized in the magazine *Woman's Day*. Why did she choose these stories about a black child? I asked her recently, and why did she purchase black dolls for my brothers and me when we were children? Because, she answered, when she went to Columbia, Missouri, as a girl to live with her cousin, she saw in a neighbor's house something she had never seen before: a black maid who was treated cruelly by the whites she worked for. "She wasn't even allowed to have her own name," my mother said. "They called her 'Hannah,' which seemed to them more like a maid's name than her actual name did. I made up my mind right then that when I had children, I would make sure they cared about colored people."

Her attraction to Little Brown Koko drew me to him as well and led me to create, with her help, my first book. This slender volume, bound by cardboard, took Koko's name as its title and contained cut-outs of all the stories she read to me. Significantly, the stories featured two characters, Koko and his mother; the father of the family is absent and never mentioned. In the only story I remember, Koko disobeys his mother by visiting the watermelon patch. As he eats a watermelon, night comes on, and for a time he can't find his way home. The little boy is not only frightened to be lost but also scared of the whipping he will get for disobeying. But when he arrives home at last, he is relieved to find that his mother speaks kindly, rather than punishing him. Racist as the story of a black boy in the watermelon patch seems to me by hindsight, this episode of Little Brown Koko ended in the very way I might have wished my own episodes of misbehavior to end. Hearing my mother, who had switched me so often, read the outcome aloud has no doubt made the story stick with me all these years. As she read it, did she wish on some level for kindness in her own childhood? Whatever her thoughts may have been, I see looking back that my book about Koko is related to the narrative poems I later wrote, some of them about people outside the social mainstream, and others about the psychological meanings of family and home.

My mother has influenced me as a poet in other ways. Today, as she answers my questions about her past, she demonstrates her knack of getting to the essence of an event or situation—for instance, explaining the injustice toward the black maid she met in Columbia through the detail of the maid being denied her own name, or conveying my grandfather's lack of feeling for his wife through the anecdote of the new broom he rested against her side of the bed on Christmas Day. To show the relentlessness of the sand that blew in north Texas during the Dust Bowl period of her childhood, my mother uses only an image. When she woke up in the morning, she says, though she had locked her window the night before, there was sand on her pillow.

And what did my father, so quickly gone from my life, contribute to me as a writer? His most obvious contribution was his disappearance itself, for it showed me once and for all that the world is a broken place, and filled me with the need to mend it. He also gave me an early regard for words, the tools I ultimately chose for the mending. At the age of three, when he worked as a journalist in Newport, New Hampshire, I imitated him by scribbling on pieces of paper to make what I thought were headlines and news articles, then taking the results around the neighborhood to sell as newspapers, in my first attempt to find readers for what I composed on a page. Could my desire to become a poet have come in part from my father, too? Did I witness moments when he read my mother a greeting card poem, or some bit of light verse for her entertainment? Though I have no memory of these things, perhaps I was aware of them as a child.

During a recent visit, spurred by my questions about her courtship with my father, my mother surprised me by producing out of the blue a poem he wrote to her in longhand shortly after they met. It took me a while to get over the shock of what she had placed in my hand, and then to consider the mystery of its existence after an interlude of seventy years. Why had she kept this poem? And why did she still have the *Better Homes and Gardens* cookbook she took it from? Carefully preserved, it was one of the cookbooks he offered as promotional gifts for potential subscribers to the magazine he was selling when he first passed through Columbia in 1938. Had she kept these things only out of her lifelong habit as a pack rat, or could she have been clinging to some residue of feeling for him all this time despite her stories of his villainy?

Written in pencil with cross-outs and faulty meter, the verse was clearly dashed off, though its comic whimsy must have appealed to my mother as a girl of seventeen.

> Some presents are to feed the mind
> With visions of above,
> Others only feed the flame
> Of constant burning love,
> But the one that we are giving you—
> We hope it's no disgrace—
> Is the kind, we hope,
> To help you feed your face.

The "we" of the poem includes its author, my father, whose name appears beneath it, and his fellow salesman, who has signed his name alongside. By involving his co-worker, perhaps my father sought to make the gift of a poem on his first meeting with my mother more acceptable. It is not a love poem, yet my father manages a reference to the flame of love on his way to the punch line, referring to his hope as well, not once but two times at the verse's conclusion. There is a sense that for this young man who has just discovered an attractive woman in Missouri, the future itself has grown more hopeful—as indeed, in the summer of 1938, it had. By early September, he would be back in Columbia before a justice of the peace to exchange wedding vows with her, and in just three years, while their love still burned, they would become my parents.

Chapter 2

The Dream of the House and Farm

> ... The woman he drew in the end
> was my mother, with her three boys, and we
>
> drew him, an odd fellow with a dangerous temper,
> who could whistle like a bird with his throat,
> and put us all to work building the house
> and farm he dreamed of ...
>
> —"Draw Me"

In one of my earliest memories, from near the end of World War II, my father told me about Hitler. A news bulletin had come on the radio about the Allied bombing of a city—perhaps Dresden—and imagining buildings engulfed by flames, I was afraid. This all happened because of Hitler, he said, and now Hitler was hiding where no one could find him.

My father's explanation did not bring me comfort. Why can't they find him? I asked over and over. After my father left the family, I associated the burning city with the destruction he himself had left behind, and as I lay in my bed longing for him, I began to confuse him with Hitler, since no one seemed able to find my father, either.

My mother certainly tried. Left alone with no child support, she had plenty of motivation to locate my father. In the late 1940s, when the Communist scare was growing in the country, she got the idea of contacting the FBI. Surely they would want to know the whereabouts of her card-carrying husband, and they had far better resources than she. Before long, two agents showed up at our door. During the course of their visit, my brother Paul remembers, both of them showed him their badges. But after they drove away, no word came about my father. In the fall of 1949 my mother decided to cut her losses and divorce him.

A year before her divorce, she was approached by a handsome bachelor named Tommy Weidler, a friend of a friend, who offered to pay her for his board. Soon Tommy became a presence at our house. My older brother Paul may be right that from time to time Tommy shared my mother's bed, and if so, I can't blame her. Left alone by a husband who had rejected her for another woman, she might well have been flattered by Tommy's advances, finding them hard to resist. I do blame her for giving him the prerogative of disciplining my brothers and me with a belt, particularly since he was a sadistic man who enjoyed toying with his power over us. In my worst memory of him, however, he did not use his belt at all. He simply dangled it in front of Johnny and me after calling us downstairs to discuss something he said we had done wrong.

"I already know what it is," he said calmly, "but if you don't lie and tell me, I won't give you the beating you deserve."

His calm expression was not reassuring. Tommy's whippings, cold and merciless, frightened us more than my mother's, and in our dread, Johnny and I began to cry. Yet we couldn't think of what we had done.

"Ask Wesley," Tommy told my brother. "He knows." And when I couldn't answer he said, "Ask Johnny."

After we were helpless with tears, my mother, who had thought the whole thing was funny, just as Tommy did, jerked his arm and got him to stop.

"We called you downstairs to give you these presents," she said, handing us a couple of Christmas gifts that had arrived late from a family relative. My traumatic memory shows that however twisted Tommy was in his authority, he and she had begun to behave as father and mother, husband and wife.

My brothers and I were not sorry when Tommy at last found a girlfriend and the boarding arrangement ceased. Not long afterward, when I was sent to the store for groceries and came up a dime short, a kindly man standing in line behind me offered the dime I needed. That event changed my family's fortunes for the rest of our stay in Southview. The good Samaritan turned out to be Springfield's town manager, who discovered after a little research that my mother was raising three children on her own. He then ordered the superintendent of the Southview projects to lower her monthly rent and set up reasonable installments for the rent she owed. Years later my mother told us there was a drawback to the arrangement. When she went to the project office with her installments, the superintendent invariably made suggestive remarks and, as she put it, "looked me up and down."

Because of the town manager's help and the goodwill of teachers, who often sent me or one of my brothers home with leftover cafeteria food, my mother was able to pay for an expensive and horrific bout of dental surgery. Photographs from my album in the middle- to late-40s reveal her problem: teeth that had begun to loosen and shift from gum disease. By 1948, when the picture was taken of her and her three sons at a picnic table, Tommy standing in the background, she smiles with front teeth that protrude at an extreme angle. The next year, when she was twenty-eight years old, a dentist told her that her gum disease was so serious her teeth would have to be extracted and replaced by dentures. The normal proce- dure, the dentist explained, was to have the upper and lower teeth removed in two separate sessions. But my mother chose to have all her teeth pulled at once. After the surgery she walked to a nearby cab stand and, unable to speak because of the numbness from novocaine and the bleeding, used hand gestures to tell a cab driver she needed a ride home.

What I remember most from the period of her recuperation is her excitement about how the dentures would alter her appearance. Her anticipation was so great it changed the atmosphere of our little apart- ment in Southview from discouragement to hope. It was as if once she had the new teeth, the family itself might somehow be able to start again. Not long after she was fitted with them, she began to do some- thing she had never done before: kiss me and my brothers goodnight as we lay in bed. "You're good boys," she would say with a happy smile that, to my eyes as I looked up at the false teeth, seemed a bit alien. In those moments she was always perfumed, lipsticked and dressed up for a date with a man she obviously cared for. Her goodnight kisses confused me, not only because as a third-grader I felt too old for them, but because the love she expressed to me seemed to be mixed with her feelings for the man she was dating. Eventually, this man became my stepfather, and my family's transformation began.

My mother met my stepfather in August of 1949, three months before her divorce was finalized, at the Duck Inn in downtown Springfield, Vermont, a beer joint frequented by my stepfather on Saturday nights. A mutual friend arranged their blind date, arriving at the Duck Inn with her own date to introduce them. Eventually my mother invited my stepfather to Southview so he could meet my brothers and me. It was a big event. At her direction we got ready for bed, dressing in the same bathrobe—a little small for us now—that we wore on the Christmas Eve when we waited in vain for our father. After my stepfather arrived, we stood in the "steps" position and sang "I'm Looking Over a Four Leaf Clover"—a popular love song we had performed years before in skits at the Southview community center, and a favorite of my father's. But we felt a little embarrassed performing the song this time. We had outgrown not only our bathrobes but our old role of the three songsters, and when Paul and I got to the verse that linked the four-leaf clover to "somebody I adore," we giggled. Looking back, I see that there were other reasons for being ill at ease—we were not only wearing the outfits we had on when my father left us, we were singing his song as a kind of audition for a man who might replace him.

What did my soon-to-be stepfather, the judge of the audition, look like? Dressed in a sport coat and string tie, Paul Joly had curly brown hair and seemed in other ways exotic. His skin was dark, a sign of the Indian blood in his family, or so he said later on. He had a straight nose and an oval face that seemed too big for his body, and his fingers were pudgy, with flat nails. We could not tell what impact our singing had on him because his face was expressionless. His mouth, partly open in concentration, gave the sense of a man asleep, an impression emphasized by his heavy eyelids, and when he spoke, as he did to compliment us briefly after our performance, his sleepy mouth made him seem, contrary to the facts, dull-witted. I eventually learned that my stepfather's family came from Quebec and he was required to use French in his father's house. Though he spoke an unaccented English that night and always used English when he lived with us, I sometimes had the sense of another grammar in his speech, and when he became upset, as we would find he often did, his sentences broke apart into disconnected words and phrases, as if in his anger, he had lost the flow of either language.

My mother must have been determined not to make the same mistakes with her second marriage that she made with her first, because my stepfather was in most ways the opposite of my father. Whereas my father was verbal—"all talk," as my mother described him—making his way in the world by inspiring others with what he said and wrote, my stepfather was never entirely comfortable with words and most at ease when working with his hands. Whereas my father disliked life on the farm, leaving my grandfather's acreage in Illinois as quickly as he could, my stepfather longed to own a piece of land where he could raise crops and plants, reminding my mother of her own farming background. And though my father made promises to my mother about the future and broke them when they became inconvenient, my stepfather proved to be faithful to his commitments. One of these was to obtain a two-year degree in horticulture before he married her so he could one day start a nursery business. Another was to use the money he had saved up while serving in the military to purchase a plot of land where he would build a house, create a small farm, and establish his nursery.

I often sketched when I was a child, and during the two years my mother waited for my stepfather to finish horticulture school at the University of New Hampshire (UNH), one of my favorite subjects was the ranch-style house with a picture window and an attached garage, the dream house of the 1950s. The inspiration for my sketches was the model my mother and stepfather had chosen in a construction magazine for their own ranch-style dwelling. It was her dream house. Until she she began to envision it in 1951, the only homes she had known were the house of her childhood in the Ozarks, which was, as she once described it to me, "nothing more than a shack," and a series of basic apartments, including the one in Southview, where she sometimes sat, entirely transported, with the construction magazine in her lap.

The location my stepfather chose for the house was thirteen acres beside the Connecticut River in West Claremont, New Hampshire, a piece of land very different from the back forty of my mother's childhood in the Ozarks of Missouri. In the Ozarks, the soil had been rocky, and roots from the trees her parents removed came back as sprouts year after year in the vegetable garden. On the land my stepfather purchased, which had been treeless since the Colonial days, there were no rocks or roots. The soil, as my stepfather proudly demonstrated in a soil map he had made for an assignment at college, was some of the most fertile in New Hampshire. In addition, the property was backed by a beautiful view of Mount Ascutney across the river in Vermont—the perfect setting for a dream house on a dream farm. "You kids are going to have to pitch in," my mother said happily, thinking less of the unceasing drudgery and confinement of her girlhood than of an ideal upbringing, in which children respected their mother and father and learned to be responsible adults by contributing to the family's common good.

My stepfather outlined his ideas about our role in the family shortly after he married my mother in 1952, the two of them just thirty years old, and he with no parental experience. He waited until he had moved us from Southview into the last of our apartments, located on the bottom floor of an old Victorian house in Claremont, New Hampshire, not far from his land alongside the Connecticut. Then, on a certain morning after breakfast in our cramped dining room, he looked up from the table with a disdainful expression we had not seen before. "From now on," he said, "things are going to be different around here." All the time he had known us, he said, we had been taking advantage of our mother, who worked every day while we just loafed. From now on, we were going to earn our room and board and learn the value of work. There would be regular chores for us, both at home and on the new property, where we would help him raise vegetables and livestock for the family. "I'll be keeping my eye on you," he said, "and if there's any funny business, you'll get the belt. You birds have been riding the gravy train long enough."

As Paul spoke, my mother sat in quiet approval at the other end of the table. She must have been gratified to have a father for her children at last, and if his appraisal of us was new to her, she was no doubt pleased by his emphasis on work and parental respect. Besides, here was a father who, contrary to her first husband, understood the importance of laying down the law. My brothers and I, on the other hand, felt betrayed. Up until this moment, we had found him pleasant and likeable—especially for the way he once took part in a game of toss and catch the three of us started with a ball of bubblegum while he was waiting for my mother to come downstairs for a date. Now we saw that even as we warmed up to him, our stepfather had been assessing our failings and our unworthiness, and planning harsh measures to deal with what he had found.

Shocked as we were by the new Paul, he had reasons for speaking as he did that morning. Like my mother, he was the oldest child in a poverty-stricken family, and his experience with cheap apartments easily matched hers. Paul's French-Canadian father, an unskilled worker in one of Claremont's several mills, moved the family to a series of run-down tenements as more and more children—six in all—were born. A violent and unfeeling man who backed up his authority with a razor strop, his father believed it was his children's duty to obey him to the letter and when they got old enough, to help him with the family's support. After they graduated one by one from eighth grade in the Catholic school, he made them quit, hand their chores down to a younger child, and find a paying job. Whatever money they brought home, he took for room and board. So when my stepfather insisted that my brothers and I earn our room and board by working on the new property, he was only telling us what his father had told him. Apart from Paul's superior officers in the military service (where he had probably learned phrases like "you birds" and "riding the gravy train"), his father was the only role model he had.

Anyway, he probably felt that he was doing better by us than his father had done by him, because he was allowing us to finish our schooling. Besides, the family house he planned would be new and modern, with far more space than any home he had lived in growing up. Stepping in to take charge of us, he would make sure we amounted to something in life, an outcome that seemed to him unlikely given our current path. Never mind that the Catholic Church had excommunicated Paul for marrying my mother, a divorced Protestant, or that his Catholic siblings refused to let their children play with my brothers and me. He would show by his skills as a farmer, house builder and father that they all had him wrong.

Troubled though my new family already was when we set out in the early 1950s, the wholesome families of American television seemed to affirm its hopeful journey. Two of the most popular shows in the period were *The Adventures of Ozzie and Harriet*, and my own favorite, *Father Knows Best*. Looking back, it is hard to see how I could have had a favorite, since we didn't have a TV and only saw the programs in the living rooms of my parents' friends during rare visits. But the rarity only sharpened my longing for the perfect family, as did my family's imperfections. I wanted to be Ricky Nelson, whose every dilemma was monitored by a solicitous mother and father. I wanted a father who always knew best, solving problems with compassion and understanding rather than the imposition of rules. It did not occur to me at the time that the rest of America wanted to live in these ideal families, too—that what made the TV shows so popular were the flaws of real-life families all around me.

No family could have been more different than mine was from the ones on TV in the 1950s. While the television dads wore suits and ties when they greeted their wives and children after their days at the office, my stepfather, whom we called by his first name (also my older brother's name), worked nights in a machine shop, rising in the afternoon to do chores dressed in T-shirts and shop pants. The TV moms, wearing blouses and skirts, whiled away their time indoors, baking, dusting and settling disputes between their offspring with a sweet goodwill. By contrast my mother, whose divorced status alone set her apart from a TV housewife, was often outdoors in dungarees on the new property—sometimes helping Paul, sometimes, with a suspicious vigilance that easily matched his, overseeing us kids as we planted and hoed the huge vegetable garden. And while the family home on television had white clapboards with an attached garage, the home we ended up in was the garage itself. Covered with tarpaper, it had wide eaves on one side, and on the other, a straight, vertical edge indicating there was more house to come—though the house was not added for several years. The large picture window Paul substituted for a garage door gave us our principal view of the world from the time I was in sixth grade until I had nearly completed high school.

Although my stepfather's house project was a protracted affair, the farm he planned quickly began to thrive. My brothers and I were fourteen, twelve and eleven in the spring of 1953, when we moved into our cramped bedroom in the tarpapered garage. Over the next two years, we raised and harvested vegetables, helped to freeze and can them, and served as the building crew for a chicken coop and most of a barn. At first the novelty of living on a farm engaged us. We liked the idea of taking care of the animals Paul purchased to complete the family's self-sufficiency—chickens, guinea hens, ducks, geese, a beef calf, pigs, and milk goats—and when plants sprouted from the rows of seeds we tamped into the riverbed soil, we were proud of our work. To set the standard for our performance and keep us motivated, Paul announced a six-month contest to determine which stepson was the best worker, offering his glow-in-the-dark wristwatch with a stainless steel bracelet as a prize. For every hour we worked, he said, he would set aside money for our college education, promising ten cents an hour extra to the stepson who was awarded the watch. At the end of the six months, I won the watch. But the bracelet gradually loosened, and the watch began falling off my wrist. Moreover, my stepfather took back his promise of college money in any amount. He couldn't afford it, he told us. Anyway, he said, he was giving us our room and board, and we should be grateful for that. As the newness of farm work wore off and we grew lax about our chores, this was a statement he repeated with growing anger.

Permitted almost no leisure time during those first summers, and working both afternoons and weekends when school was in session, we came to see our life in West Claremont as an endless grind. It didn't help that Paul took to addressing us as "hammerheads" or "jugheads" when we displeased him, sometimes cuffing us in the head. For serious infractions, he led us into his and my mother's bedroom and used his belt. "Lower your drawers," he would say. We bent over the bed with our pants and underwear around our ankles, and each time he swung his belt he reminded us of the chores we had forgotten or our bad attitude, finishing only after our legs were striped with red and he was out of breath.

When we kids joined Paul on a group project, he sometimes flung himself into the work with no sense of our limits or his. Once he stood on the top of the stud wall he had erected for the barn and dangled a loading hook while my brothers and I lifted a rafter far too heavy for us, dropping it over and over. During the fall a year later, after he had started the family well with the help of a professional well-digger, he set up his own operation for digging and drafted my older brother as his helper. Tying the rope to the front bumper of his pickup truck, Paul threaded it through a pulley on a tripod he had positioned over the well, then perhaps 40 feet deep, attaching the rope to a mud bucket. Then he sat in the driver's seat of his truck with the door open and started the engine. "See that bucket hanging over the well?" he asked my brother. "I'm going to be standing on it while you lower me down with my shovel." Paul demonstrated how to put the truck into first gear and let the clutch out while slowly applying the gas. As the truck moved slowly forward, the bucket began to descend. Then Paul put the truck into reverse, lifting the bucket and resting it on the well's platform. "That's how you're going to raise me back up," he explained. He got out of the truck so my brother could try it. "T-N-T," he said, flipping his right hand theatrically as if to swat a pesky fly. "T'aint Nothin' To it."

It didn't seem so easy to my brother, who, at age fifteen, had never driven a vehicle before. After stalling the engine two or three times, he was finally able to coordinate the clutch and the gas, though I could see how nervous he was. When Paul stood up on the bucket with his shovel and signaled my older brother to begin, I was nervous, too. I still remember Paul swaying back and forth on the bucket as he rose or descended, and swearing at my brother for jerking the rope. But after a while the system seemed to work. I stepped in to help, waving to my brother when Paul reached the bottom of the well, and waving again when he had filled the bucket and was ready to come out.

Then things went terribly wrong. Leaning over the well with me so he could hear our stepfather's order to raise the bucket, my older brother loosened one of the boards from the platform and sent it straight down. "I'm sorry!" he shouted. "It was an accident!" But when Paul began to curse him more angrily than ever, my brother flew into a rage himself. One by one, he hurled the remaining boards down into the well. That was the moment Johnny and I took off for our bedroom to hide out until the conflict blew over.

A half-hour later our older brother walked in wearing a triumphant smile.

"What happened to Paul?" I asked him.

"I don't know where he is," he replied. "He got back out of the well, though. I went to do my chores in the root cellar, and after I carried a load of cabbages down the ladder, there he was," my brother said. "He started pegging cabbages at me from the pile and hollering, 'How do you like having things thrown down at you, you little son-of-a-bitch, you?' I dodged them all just by backing away from the opening. After he was gone, I climbed back up the ladder and left them there."

"How did he ever get out of the well?" Johnny wanted to know.

Suddenly there was a loud crack above our heads. We looked up astonished as the ceiling opened and our stepfather fell out of it, landing at our feet on the bedroom floor. Not until he stood up, brushed the sheetrock off himself in embarrassment, and walked out of our bedroom did we realize the significance of what had taken place. My brother's unpredicted anger at the well had sparked Paul's suspicion that we three were plotting against him. Crawling into the space above the room to listen in on us, he was trying to find out how deep our conspiracy went.

Paul's bizarre and ill-fated career as a spy suggests he was aware of growing feelings in his stepsons that his strict rules could not accommodate. Nevertheless, the only change he made was to the ceiling. When we returned from school the next day, the two sections of sheetrock that had hung open were once more sealed by nails as if nothing had happened. Afterward, Paul dedicated himself even more firmly to his rules, and to enforcing them with his belt.

The endless rounds of work in West Claremont continued as well. "You'll never get anywhere," Paul told us, "until you learn the meaning of work." After the harvest was done in the fall, he had us cutting down trees along the riverbank for firewood. On weekends during the winter, he took us to the nearby paper mill, where we all shoveled cinders to level the driveway. None of us worked harder than my mother. Each night after she served dinner and Paul left for the shop, she sat at her sewing machine mending or sewing clothes until the wee hours of the morning. "Sleep is for people who have nothing better to do," she said. Like my stepfather, she was raised during the Depression and had substituted work for play throughout her childhood. Like him, she was used to denying herself what she desired. If their shared dream of happiness along the Connecticut required them to give up happiness, they were prepared to do so for as long as it took.

From a night in the early 1950s, this concluding memory. While my mother works the pedal of her sewing machine and clips thread with her scissors, I lie in my bed listening to a dramatization on "Lux Radio Theater" of the movie *Shane*, which plays on the console by her side. The radio program is wondrous to me, interweaving American dream life and my own experience in ways I don't quite understand but am eager to know.

The program tells the story of a young boy and his parents who build a new homestead in a Western valley and are befriended by a cowboy named Shane. Arriving out of nowhere one day on his horse, Shane stays on to help with the work of the house and the farm. In the weeks that follow, they transform the place unbelievably from its unpromising beginnings, uprooting trees and erecting fences and outbuildings for their increasing herd of cattle. In the meantime the boy, Joey, learns practical skills and comes to admire Shane—more than ever after Chris Ryker shows up with the Ryker gang to run the family off its farm, and Shane fights him to the ground with his fists. Compared to his ordinary father Shane is, for Joey, a magical figure, and by the end of the show, when Shane clears all the gunslingers from the valley and departs on his horse toward the Western mountains, Joey seems devoted to him alone. "Shane" he calls again and again, "Come back."

What meaning this radio program, with its American dream of house and farm, has for my mother, who listens quietly as she works, I do not even consider. Though she is awake with me on this night in the tarpapered garage-house of our valley farm, I have become that boy who cries out with the desire to leave his family and its limited dream and go where life is more open and true and just. Yet even as I call to the man who might take me there, this dream father so unlike the stepfather I have been given, he has disappeared, just as my absent father once disappeared, the two of them all along nothing more than mist.

Chapter 3

The West Claremont Self

Once, as the teenage boy walked up
and down the gutter with the wide blade
of a shovel above his head, and the goats
turned toward him in their stalls
undoing with their blats the band
music he held in his mind,

his stepfather, who had only asked,
for Christ's sake, to have the barn
cleaned out, rested his hand
on his hip in the doorway.
The boy would not have guessed
when he marched in his first parade

that he carried the flag for his stepfather,
or for his angry mother, also raised
for work and self-denial
during the Depression. . . .

—"The Boy Carrying the Flag"

A year before I lay in bed listening to *Shane*, as my family and I commuted back and forth from the Broad Street apartment to my stepfather's acreage in West Claremont, I began to write and illustrate a series of books. My goal, as I saw it then, was to entertain young children with fantastical stories. Rereading the books today in the scrapbook where they have been stored away, I discover that my underlying aim was to tell my own story, using the events I imagined to address the family situation in which I found myself. These early volumes, one of a kind, were called "Tot Books," and three of them comprised "The Sky Series," featuring characters who long for a better life and journey through an alternative world in the sky to find it. The better life they seek always involves a new home. One of the characters is a lost helium balloon, accidentally set adrift by a child, which floats its way into a number of misadventures, eventually ending up in the hands of the very child who lost it. The delighted child then takes the balloon to the home of a loving mother and father, where it lives "happily ever after." In another book Susie, a Jeep who yearns for a home in heaven, drives to the Pearly Gate and seeks entry. Is she worthy of this home she wishes for, given her past life? There is such concern about her possible unworthiness that a court trial must be held to decide her fate. In the end the judge absolves her, and she enters the Pearly Gates to spend eternity with the angels, chauffeuring them among the clouds.

The third story in the Sky Series concerns a toy watch whose name, significantly enough, is Wesley. Once again the theme is unworthiness, since Wesley is a "cheap, ten-cent" wristwatch who wants more than anything else to become a "professional" watch that tells time, like the ones in his pin-ups—the pictures he has hung of Bulovas, Hamiltons, and Gruens. His unsympathetic owner Jimmy accuses him of having "a blank look" and "no brains" (accusations originating with my mother and stepfather) and one day threatens to throw him away.

That night a spirit appears to guide Wesley skyward to the headquarters of Father Time, a gentle and compassionate father, who transforms him into a working watch and takes him to meet the watches pictured in his pin-ups.

Here, just when the story seems poised for a happy ending, things start to go wrong for Wesley. He tires of the never-ending process of moving his hands to tell time, and he can't stand the noise of his own ticking. Now what Wesley wants is his old self back, never mind the taunts and threats of his owner, Jimmy. When he wakes up to discover he has only dreamed his transformation into a professional watch, he is overjoyed. One by one, he takes down the pin-ups from his wall. The story of Wesley the wristwatch becomes a tale of self-affirmation.

This unexpected turn did not come without help. My brother Paul, an aspiring writer himself, suggested that Wesley take the pictures down from his wall as a way of dramatizing his self-acceptance. Looking back, I am amazed to think of the two of us, who struggled with our own feelings of unworthiness in that West Claremont home years ago, collaborating on how best to show Wesley's realization of his worth. At age twelve, I was impressed by our collaboration, too. So I wrote with my best printing in the front of *The Adventures of a Wrist Watch* this dedication: "To Paul, without whose help this book would not have been possible."

My mother liked the writing and illustrations of the Sky Series so much that she preserved them with other memorabilia in my scrapbook. She didn't suspect any more than I did their clues about our family's dysfunction, to which she made her own continuing contribution. Every bit as negative as my stepfather's words jughead and hammerhead were the nicknames she invented for us. Because my brother John was, in her view, "always frowning," he was "Frowny." Paul was overly assertive and assured—"just like your father," she would tell him. His nickname was "Big Shot." I was "Sneaky," the kid who tried to get around the family's rules and regulations. We never quite knew when she would slap us for the weaknesses after which we had been named. If the time came for more than a slap—for, that is, a whipping by my stepfather—she was the one who made the decision. When one of us talked back, she might say, "I haven't liked your attitude for the past week," or catching us getting into the graham crackers for a snack: "You knew damn well you weren't supposed to take those, and you went right ahead and did it." Her tone alone said that Paul would be waiting for us after school the next day with his belt. I will never forget the anxiety I felt on bus rides home about his whippings.

Yet I also recall the moment when, in her enthusiasm for *The Adventures of a Wrist Watch*, my mother took the book to my stepfather. "You ought to read this story Wesley wrote," she says to him, "it's really good." Night has come to our apartment on Broad Street in this moment, and as I lie in bed, I watch her through the half-open door that leads to the living room, offering him the book. "Maybe later," Paul replies, returning to his newspaper. She stands there awhile longer in silence, then turns away. In her disappointment I sense her love, as I sense it now, mixed as that love was with unreasonable expectations, heartless punishment, and her own inherited feelings of unworthiness. As for Paul, whom she made uncomfortable by her question, love was never part of the contract he announced when he became the father in our family, any more than it was a guiding principal for his own father. The only evidence of a bond with him I could claim was the wristwatch he had given me for my work—the watch that must have been somewhere in my mind, and was perhaps even on my wrist, as I wrote my story.

In my mother's photo album there are only a few family snapshots from my youth in West Claremont. One shows a stack of well tiles in our new backyard, from the period of my stepfather's well-digging. Another offers a front view of the garage, with its picture window and cut-off right side. Set against a barren landscape in late fall, it seems the loneliest dwelling ever photographed. Two other photos show me and my brothers with shovels in a lengthening trench where pipes would be laid from the house to the riverbank. The captions are "Digging" and "and Digging." Most of the other snapshots from the period are loose or in envelopes. That is because by then, my mother had lost interest in my photo album. My stepfather had purchased a slide camera and projector, a popular combination in homes all over America during the mid-1950s. Now our family took to the screen, in shows attended by my parents' friends or relatives. As with the photographs in the album, nearly all of these pictures were taken by my mother and present the legend of our new family, with no sign of its difficulties. My brother Paul recently transferred some of the slides to paper, showing him, me and Johnny transformed by life in rural New Hampshire. We lift hay with our pitchforks into the pickup truck, harvest potatoes, and display prize-winning vegetables at the Cornish Fair. In a photo shot behind the garage, we are making concrete for the foundation of the house. While the three of us stand with our shovels beside a gravel pile, my stepfather pours the contents of a cement mixer into his wheelbarrow, smiling for the camera.

I must have just turned fourteen, because at the right of the photograph is a baby standing up in a carriage watching us: my sister Karen, born early in 1955. Another snapshot, taken when Karen was still an infant, shows the whole family seated together all dressed up, Karen in my mother's lap. What is most noticeable in this photograph, besides how cramped we are in the garage on our short couch, is my mother's happiness. Her obvious pleasure in the company of her new daughter makes me realize that the expressions I mostly saw on her face growing up were those of tension and distress. My mother's happy smile in the picture squares with the light-heartedness I recall in my home during her pregnancy in my thirteenth year, the family buoyed by the anticipation of Karen's birth. That was the year my mother bought art supplies just before Christmas and asked me to paint Mary and the Christ child on the garage window with Joseph and the animals surrounding them, a family scene that must have been especially resonant for her in her sixth month. It was also the year I got permission to bring my art teacher home and show him the mirrors my mother had painted with landscape views and hung in our living room. After my sister was born in March, the only crying that came from my parents' bedroom was from Karen, and because she was a beautiful child with whom my brothers and I were instantly smitten, the crying was tolerable, even welcome.

As it happened, I was also smitten in the spring of 1955 with Carol Diamond, a girl in junior choir. Our relationship came to a head on the night of our shared performance at the high school graduation in Claremont, just after my fourteenth birthday. Though I was supposed to wait for my mother to pick me up after graduation was over, I walked for the first time hand in hand with my girlfriend to the playground behind my old elementary school, where the two of us talked for an hour or two, held each other, and kissed. Giddy with love, I walked her back to her house and started home, becoming convinced during the five miles of my journey that my mother would understand why I hadn't shown up for my ride. Surely, I told myself, she herself had been in love just like me in her past; she would see how my feeling had led me astray. But when I got home and tried my hopeful argument, she was enraged.

"What is wrong with your head?" she shouted. "You sneak off with some girl and leave me waiting for you, and now you're trying to make it my fault? Get to bed. You haven't heard the end of this, Mister."

The punishment my parents announced the next day was worse than a whipping. There would be no more contact with Carol Diamond. I was grounded for the summer, with extra chores to keep me occupied, just in case I had the idea of sneaking off again.

That was when I ran away in my mind. I went through the motions of my work as if I were somewhere else, eating and speaking little.

Whenever there was an odd bit of spare time, I spent it with a sketch-book in my hand, making drawings and writing rhymed poems that I showed to no one. Once I picked up an issue of *U.S. News &World Report*, the news magazine my stepfather subscribed to, and tucked it into my sketchbook. The issue featured the lost prisoners of war in North Korea, and I became preoccupied with their incarceration, unconsciously linking it to mine. "You were like a stone with eyes," my older brother tells me today. "Nobody could reach you," he adds. That was not quite true. When my mother called me a lamebrain and my stepfather said I was "not all there," I both heard and half believed them, unaware of my psychological condition. I understand now that my behavior was my first episode of a deep dissociation, or "numbing out." By becoming a stone, I made myself invulnerable to the trauma of my family life. This is why a closer look at the snapshot of my family on the couch in 1955 reveals that despite my mother's happiness about her new daughter, I wear no expression, and why, posing alone with vegetables in another photo, I am absent-eyed and desperately thin.

During the Carol Diamond summer my brother Paul, my princi-pal confidante, went to work at a goat farm in Lyme, Vermont, where he was given room and board, and his departure enforced my mental retreat. No doubt the punishment our dog Socks received made its own contribution. Socks, a pound dog to whom I was deeply attached, had never seen ducks before, and shortly after my stepfather brought home a flock, she attacked one of them, tearing the feathers off its back and wounding it so deeply the duck had to be killed. My stepfather's approach, rather than penning the ducks up so the dog couldn't get at them, was to beat the dog so brutally she would never go near them again. Watching that dog, overpowered and howling as she struggled against him, I felt every blow myself.

Though I kept the photo of Carol Diamond she gave to me and looked at it often, we weren't able to sustain our relationship that fall, when I entered my freshman year. I was always needed for work after school and on weekends, and she, for her part, was mysteriously inacces-sible. As an adult, I learned that in her adolescence, she suffered periods of mental illness, all hidden beneath the 1950s optimism of Claremont, New Hampshire. Later on I discovered the trouble other high school friends endured, even as I envied them their normalcy and contentment. The mother of one, longing for an exotic life, dated and slept with salesmen she met through her job at a local motel. Another watched both her parents fall steadily into alcoholism as she was growing up. Claremont was, after all, not very well suited to optimism, being a mill town of immigrants who had known the sorrows of the Depression and World War II. But during the decade of the happy families on American television, with their laugh tracks and cheerful outcomes, all families put on a good front. None of my friends would have guessed my own problems as a teenager at home—for instance, that I faced my stepfather's belt each time I brought home a report card with a C on it, or that in my first week of ninth grade, I was whipped on three consecutive afternoons for forgetting my lunchbox at school.

How could I have forgotten the lunchbox three times running, denied lunches until I brought it home? My parents were both displeased and dumbfounded. The first time I came home without it, they got angry; the second time they shook their heads; the third time, my mother actually smiled, my cluelessness was so unbelievable.

"Have you lost your mind?" she asked. "When are you going to get your head out of the clouds and come back down to earth?"

Paul was less mystified, explaining my problem with his usual expression for my failings: hammerhead. As for me, all I could offer was that I didn't mean to do it.

None of us understood that each successive beating created a dissociation in my mind that made me more likely to forget my lunchbox than to remember it. Nor did we see that the lunchbox was a symbol of the self that I wanted to dispense with. By carrying it around and eating out of it while the kids in my new school ate cafeteria food, I was declaring myself a "farmer," which was the name my 1950s peers gave to classmates from rural areas outside Claremont who were impossibly uncool. My identity as a farmer was the very thing I wanted to hide, since it was connected with the shameful sense of self that had begun when I was a child in Southview and continued to develop on the farm in West Claremont. Forgetting the lunchbox meant that for the time being I did not have to carry the object that threatened to expose who I "really was" to my classmates and to the world.

Year by year as I attended high school, the split between my West Claremont and Claremont selves grew more extreme. Elected as a freshman to the student council, I experienced the approval of my peers, and I craved more of it. By the end of that year, when I was selected for the senior choir and picked, because of my height, to carry the American flag in the color guard, my high school identity had become a compulsion for me, proof that I was not unlovable after all, and at the same time a cover for the shameful and unlovable self I feared was the real me. Student council membership was not enough: I wanted to become president of my class.

How could I make this happen? I asked my brother Paul in the weeks before the start of my sophomore year. He had just returned from a week at the New Hampshire Boys' State Conference, where he learned by study and practice the art of political campaigning. Once I got myself nominated for president, he advised, all I had to do was nominate my competitors on the ballot for other class offices, too, thereby dispersing their votes in the election. His method worked, and for each of the next three years I was class president. Given that my classmates elected me to the student council as a freshman and a sophomore, I might well have had enough support in my bid for class president without manipulating the vote. By guaranteeing the result, I ultimately turned my success into a source of guilt, for behind the story of my social acceptance was the secret story of the one who didn't deserve it.

To keep up the appearance of a cool cat, as the most popular males in my high school were called, I had to dress the part. This was a challenge, however, since my brothers and I got our clothes from church rummage sales in Claremont, and what we found there were mostly cast-offs from families as hard up as ours: old ties, suit coats with wide lapels and enormous shoulder pads, and shirts that had floppy collars and worn elbows. Failing to find the sun-tans and button-down plaids that the coolest of my peers wore, I chose the next-best thing: outrageous apparel that would attract the eye, deflecting attention from my size fourteen wing tip shoes. One of my proudest discoveries was a silk vest with dragons on it. It was too short, but that was a small drawback for the effect it gave. I also picked out a pair of brown tweed trousers flecked with green, red, and orange, whose outlandishness had a cost since they were itchy and loose around the waist. Nonetheless, they were my favorite pants, and I wore them cinched tight with a belt even on the hot days of early fall and late spring.

Reviewing the photos my brother Paul has made from slides, I discover with amusement another of my favorites, as close to the style of the period as I could muster: a gray sweater, much too short, which I proudly wore with a black shirt, though it was not a button-down. In the snapshot the shirt's collar is so large it can't be tucked in, and it spreads out like crows' wings. Wearing that sweater or my dragon vest, I boarded the school bus in the early morning with my brothers and made the long trip through the back roads toward Claremont as the bus picked up other country kids. A few of them were from affluent families, but most wore hand-me-down clothes and stood outside jerry-built houses. They were, in short, kids just like me, though I was loathe to admit the resemblance, on my way to my transformation as a member of the popular clique at the high school. On the ride home, I always chose a window seat so I could wave at my classmates from town as they walked down Pleasant Street. After they passed from view, I wondered about the impression I had left with them. Did my wave and smiling face help to sustain my popularity, even though I was on my way to West Claremont and unable to walk with them?

Meanwhile, in West Claremont, a rebellion was brewing. My older brother figured out that if he tightened the muscles on his legs when Paul whipped him, it didn't hurt. "Just don't bend over when he belts you. Stand up straight like this," he said, crossing his arms and firming his buttocks and legs. Next time my stepfather called me into the bedroom, I tried it, too. By then, he had a new refrain as he swung his belt. "You're no damn good," he would say, and "You'll never be worth a shit." But as I stood there taking his whipping, neither the belt nor his words hurt me. Suddenly I turned around and faced him, taller now than he was, and my own words jumped from my mouth. "When I grow up," I said, "I intend to become a self-respecting human being."

Paul was as surprised as I was. "Oh, yeah?" he finally said. Then the whipping stopped. Though my family misfortune was not yet over, my stepfather never beat me again.

My older brother's rebellion culminated a few months later, in the fall of 1957, when he packed up his belongings early one morning and left home. Later on he went to live with my father in Chicago, overthrowing my mother's orthodoxy of my father as a villain, and turning her and my stepfather against him. Consequently they avoided using Paul's name in our house. The bad news for me in the fallout was that I no longer had a confidante I could seek out in times of distress. The good news was that there was less distress. Evidently fearing I might leave home myself, my parents loosened their control over me. The summer before my brother left, my stepfather had decided what summer work I would have, volunteering me for a job on a farm in Cornish, New Hampshire. In the summer of 1958, however, when I applied for a job as kitchen help at Lost River Gorge in the White Mountains, neither of them objected.

In the fall of my senior year, I even began to "go steady" with a girl named Pat Bouvier. Pat was the French and Catholic daughter of a couple known to my stepfather, and through a girlfriend she sent me the message that she thought I was, as the expression went, "cute." Pat was, to my eyes, not just cute but beautiful, with long brown hair, full lips, and hazel eyes. I could hardly believe it when we were holding hands on our first walk together, from her parents' small apartment on the third floor of a triple-decker in Claremont to the nearby paper mill that employed her father and many of his French Catholic neighbors.

At the paper mill she wanted to turn back, and as we reached her street again, she withdrew her hand from mine. It turned out that her mother didn't approve of holding hands, since this might lead to sin. Nor did she permit long walks, or regular ones. On the one day of the week I was allowed to stay after school and visit Pat, the two of us usually sat in her living room watching, under a cross, Dick Clark's TV show *American Bandstand*, where other teenage couples danced and held each other. Meanwhile her mother, a thin woman with the sallow skin of a heavy smoker, sat nearby in the kitchen, chain-smoking and chatting intimately with her caged monkey. Sometimes Mrs. Bouvier flipped through catalogs to show me the clothes she'd ordered for Pat, her only child. "Pat didn't like the skirt at first," she would say to me, "but I just love the way it goes with this sweater, don't you?" Once a barber specially hired to cut Pat's hair turned up. "Where's that beautiful girl of yours, Mrs. Bouvier?" he asked, knowing this would please her. Then he opened his case of combs, scissors and thinning shears, and the session began, Pat holding a mirror, the barber explaining how each change would enhance her good looks, and her mother standing at Pat's side to assess the overall effect.

Before supper Pat's mother would always drive me home, and after the first couple of months, I was allowed to join the two of them on the bench seat in front, beside Pat. Our lips never once touched. In fact, this was the closest Pat ever got to me, or I to her. Looking back, I see that she lived in her own 1950s compound, caged like her mother's monkey. At the time, though, frustrated as I was that I could never be alone with her, I felt on my dates a sense of freedom akin to the freedom I had known the previous summer at Lost River. During the fall, when the pop music charts were full of the rock 'n' roll music I loved, I even trained at the local radio station to be a disc jockey. For the first time I sensed a connection between the life I was living and the wishes I had for myself.

My feeling of connection came to an abrupt end one night in early November when choir practice got over early at the high school. A friend offered to drive my brother Johnny and me to a new soda shop at the edge of town, and we agreed. After all, our parents would not arrive to pick us up for several minutes, we reasoned; we would make a quick trip and they would never know. But by the time we returned to the school, they had come and gone.

Repeating my experience of years before when I missed my ride to be with Carol Diamond, I walked the five miles home, concocting with Johnny the unlikely story that the high school principal had asked us and some other members of the choir to drop in at his house after practice. Our parents didn't buy it, and when my mother, smelling mendacity, called the principal and discovered our story didn't check out, they decided to hold me responsible as the older son who should have known better. With whippings by then out of the question, my parents grounded me, as they had done after my unapproved date with Carol Diamond. This time the grounding was for the eight remaining months of my senior year.

I wasn't especially upset that the grounding took away my weekly visits with Pat Bouvier. Since her mother was our constant chaperone, our dates were a dead end anyway. What bothered me was that dating of any kind was over until my graduation, as were all my extracurricular activities—choir, color guard, and class office—the very means by which I had managed to escape my West Claremont self. Seeing there was no way for me to save my place in the choir or the color guard, I silently resolved I would not give up being president of the senior class. Instead I would hold my class meetings during school hours and keep them a secret from my parents, which I managed to do for the entire year, maintaining in this way my claim on the "good" self I had constructed in the face of my unworthiness.

In December 1958, near the middle of my senior year in high school, the family moved from the garage into the new house. My sister Karen recalls only the excitement and ruckus of the move. This, she says, is her very first memory, more about a feeling than what really happened. No doubt that feeling originated with my mother, who looks back on the move as a crowning event in her life. She speaks of the "miracle" of the extremely mild winter day which allowed my stepfather to remove the large pane of the garage's picture window and fit it into the frame he had prepared in our new living room. "It was as if the whole thing was meant to be," she says. I myself have no memory of anything that happened on that day. But of course the move had a different meaning for me. Several years earlier I had completed drawings of our house-to-be as a dream home that would transform my family's life. But the house where my family now took up residence seemed to me a kind of jail for which my parents, the jailers, had thrown away the key.

I responded to my grounding and the extra work that went with it just as I had before in the face of family stress—by psychological numbing and depression. Despite my helplessness, however, I found ways to rebel. I did my chores at the slowest speed possible. When my stepfather grew angry about my slowness and swung his fists at me, I raised my own fists in warning, blocking his. My parents had already given me their worst punishment with the grounding, I told myself, so what did I have to lose? By the spring of 1959, I had had enough. Like my brother Paul, I ran away from home.

I made my escape in three, deliberate steps. First, I brought my guitar to school under some pretext and gave it to my English teacher, Mr. Paquette, who agreed to hold it for me until I came for it later on. That night I hid some extra clothes in the grass beside the mailbox where the school bus stopped. The next day I boarded the bus with the clothes, and when the school day was over, I took another bus to my friend Chris

Woodward's house. Chris's father justified putting me up with words similar to those of Mr. Paquette. "If you were my son, I would want to know someone treated you well until the conflict at home was resolved," he said.

Two weeks later, when I still didn't want to live at home, Chris drove me there to pick up more of my things, and my stepfather walked out to the driveway. "Your mother is very upset about this," he said. "If you come back, we'll take you off your punishment."

Surprised by how subdued and contrite he was, I decided after one more overnight at Chris's house to return. For a whole month, the atmosphere at home was harmonious. During "senior week," a time of partying and celebration that preceded graduation at my high school, my parents let me come and go as I chose. But gradually they seemed to resent the very peace my stepfather had negotiated, and discord set in all over again. After one last eruption of my stepfather's temper, I left home for good.

It is clear to me now that what truly liberated me in that period of conflict and well beyond it was my reading and my writing. Sometime in the fall of my senior year I received a small but heavy box in the mail from John Huot. John, a student at Columbia University, was a guide on the staff at Lost River, and I had written and shared poems with him and another guide and college student named George Ingraham during the previous summer—my first attempts in free verse. The box John sent from New York City was an extraordinary gift. It contained novels by William Faulkner, Ernest Hemingway, John Dos Passos, Carson McCullers, Jack Kerouac, and Alexander Solzhenitsyn; plays by Bertolt Brecht and Arthur Miller; collections of essays by R. P. Blackmur and Randall Jarrell; and most important, poetry by Cummings, Ferlinghetti, Sandburg, Frost, Williams, and Eliot. Poring over these volumes at age seventeen in rural New Hampshire, I got a sense of the modern tradition in America that would otherwise have taken years to acquire. And reading the literary magazine from Columbia that John had included, containing poems he himself had written, I began to imagine I might one day publish my own poetry.

Some of the books John sent related closely to my situation in rural New Hampshire. In the opening of Carson McCullers's *Ballad of the Sad Café*, I found a description of a decaying mill town that reminded me of my own mill town of West Claremont. My town, too, was "lonesome, sad, and like a place . . . far off and estranged from all the other places of the world." The images of failing farms in Robert Frost's *Selected Poems* touched on the agrarian decay I had seen along the Connecticut River. William Faulkner also wrote of rural decay, and in his novels *The Sound and the Fury* and *The Hamlet*, I learned about families that, like my own, had nothing to do with the ones I saw on 1950s TV—families even more dysfunctional than mine. Eventually, these writers and many of the others would influence my techniques and views as a writer.

In the meantime, isolated on my stepfather's farm, I studied the books John Huot sent to me and wrote more poems. In the cauldron of loneliness, pain and rage in West Claremont, I began my transformation into an artist.

Chapter 4

The Need to Be a Writer

... Each day

on Kuhre's farm the cows walked slowly
out into the fields in their dream
of going out into the fields and each night
they dreamed of me waving my skinny arms

calling them back to the whitewashed
cobwebby barn, as I call them now,
latching them in their long rows of stalls
where they bawl for grain, and the tangled
barn cats cry for milk, and the milking machine
begins its great breathing and sighing

in the twilight ...

—"Kuhre's Farm"

On a night in November sometime after I've started this memoir, my wife Diane, my son Sean, and I visit my mother at her house in West Claremont, rebuilt after a fire that damaged it several years ago. Around us are stacks of the things she rescued: gray sheets of paper, charred magazines, and books still swollen by water from the fire hoses. Some of the books lie on the floor beneath bricks for what she calls "pressing." She doesn't notice the burn smell her rescued belongings give off all this time later, and she is used to stepping around the piles of newspapers, bags of clothes, and old mail strewn around the house. When I tell her I will hire someone to clean up the clutter, she snaps, "This is not clutter. I've set these things aside to sort through them when I have the time. How would anybody else know what to save?"

My mother, in short, is a saver, and tonight she is sorting through a small, metal trunk she's dragged out of the closet. At last she holds up an ancient paper bag. "This has your name on it, so it must belong to you. It's been in there for so long, I almost forgot I had it," she says. "It even survived the fire."

She has no memory of the first thing I pull out of the bag, but I remember it well. It is the wrapping from a small package sent to me long ago by her sworn enemy, my father. Inside the package, which bore no card or letter, I once discovered a present for my birthday when I turned fifteen: a wristwatch.

I am surprised not only by the wrapping, but by the fact she has saved it. As I unfold it to get a better view of the address label bordered in red and blue, I think of the odd connection in my boyhood between wristwatches and fathers—first the watch with the metal bracelet my stepfather awarded me for my work as a child and later, this one. "Do you remember the watch that came in the package?" I ask my mother. She doesn't recall either the watch or the package. Nor does she remember the book she once recommended to my stepfather about a wristwatch named Wesley, who left the earth to find a compassionate Father Time in the clouds.

I reach back into the bag to discover a second, smaller bag, and when I open that one I'm even more surprised by what I find. In my hands is the manuscript of poetry I wrote at age seventeen and have long assumed was lost.

One by one I turn the handwritten pages, reliving the anticipation I felt as I lay in bed at night during the misery of my senior year. Outside my room, meanwhile, my mother sat typing from this manuscript my first volume of poetry. Unable to type myself, I asked her to do it, knowing she would understand the manuscript's importance to me, just as she had understood my Little Brown Koko and Tot Books, which she also put aside and saved. After she inserted the typed pages into the plastic sleeves of an album—my book—and gave it to me, I misplaced it. But my mother had not lost the original, even though she doesn't recognize it now, when I show her.

Which is to say that though she caused me much pain and suffering in my childhood and youth, my mother was also an ally in my development as a writer. Was I seeking her love when I presented her with this manuscript for typing back then? Probably so, and I no doubt saw the work she did on my book as an expression of her love. Yet it is not enough to assign my development as a poet to the psychological struggles of a victim. I believe that I was shaped not only by family crisis but by my own impulse as a writer, an impulse so strong that I "wrote" newspapers at age three, and was known as the class poet all through elementary school.

The author Ross Macdonald, linking conflicts like mine in early life to the writing impulse, refers to "a peculiar distancing, which generally occurs in childhood or youth and makes the direct satisfactions of living unsatisfactory, so that one has to seek one's basic satisfactions indirectly through what we can loosely call art. What makes the verbal artist," MacDonald says, "is some kind of shock or crippling or injury which puts the world at one remove from him, so that he writes about it to take possession of it." In the end, I think, the crisis of my growing-up years fueled my need to become a writer, making my life as a poet inevitable. Moreover, through the cycles of rejection and reaching out for approval in my boyhood, I toughened myself for the rounds of rejection, self-imposed and otherwise, that are common to the writing life, preparing myself for that life in the way many other writers have likely prepared themselves. This is the affirmative side of my story. Awkward and disoriented though I sometimes appeared to my parents and even to myself, I was on this deeper level coming into focus, as my early manuscript shows. How, then, am I to think about the troubles of my childhood and youth? Despite the unhappiness they once caused me, they sometimes seem to me a kind of gift, a source of my artistic development.

My mother took a long time to complete my typewritten book of poems, stalling and dangling me at every turn in response to my transgressions, real or imagined, as was her habit. Yet even though she did not stint in criticizing me, she never criticized the poetry itself, just reproduced its unconventional capitalization and punctuation as she found it, together with the poems' occasionally erotic content. Perhaps she respected my prerogatives as a developing writer because she recalled her own writing as a college student when she was my age; or maybe she knew that serious as I was about my writing, I wouldn't have changed the poems even if she had objected.

The record shows that I made none of the changes suggested by my senior English teacher, Mr. Paquette, whose commentary runs throughout the manuscript in a bold and confident script. "I resent the 'you' in poetry," he says about a poem that addresses the reader, adding later on, "You could produce the same effect by words other than 'and.'" Beneath those criticisms the seventeen year old writes—to himself, having no one else to address—that his teacher has missed the poem's objective, and its "emotive content." In the margins of the manuscript are also instructions to my mother for her typing of my free verse, such as "cap's are in black," "no cap's anywhere," and "spacing through here important." A third set of notes is devoted to self-criticism, showing I was not afraid to be hard on myself, even though I brushed aside my teacher's comments. "Prosaic and clumsy—fix this," I wrote, and later, "too abstruse— no transitions—very poor."

What strikes me about these notes today is their combination of self-assurance and determination, qualities also embodied by the poems' experimentation. In them, I explored a variety of poetic styles and subjects derived from the books John Huot sent me, adapting what I found to my own needs. Here is a poem, for instance, that personifies night as it arrives in the streets of a town and departs the next day:

> Tall clumsy dark,
> stumbling over the buildings
> and falling into the road
> and getting up, brushing off his big, black coat.
>
> Arguing with the street lamps
> he cursing in hard syllables of black
> and shouting night
>
> He walking along the street
> and forgetting evening
> in the alleys . . . . . .
>
> And remembering it, coming
> back for it in the morning

The town I had in mind was Claremont, New Hampshire, as it might have appeared to me at evening while thumbing a ride home after a school meeting, or looking out the window of the returning band bus after an away game. My literary inspiration for the poem was T. S. Eliot's "Love Song of J. Alfred Prufrock," which opens with the metaphor of a yellow fog that comes at evening and slides along the streets and alleyways.

For other poems in my manuscript I borrowed the typography of e. e. cummings, as in this excerpt from a poem about a northern New England snowfall.

> white earth
>   lay dreaming of
>   soft
>   somethings
>   asking
>   something
> (but it was impossible to know what). . . .

Reading Cummings, my teenage libido in full flourish, I was delighted to discover his erotic poems. So I tried some of my own, writing in this excerpt about a shared sexual climax, even though in real life I had experienced no such thing:

> How can we be this
> (turned inside out)
> fiercely a soft somehow bubble

I wrote about people at the fringes of society in my manuscript, too, among them a war-damaged beggar. His plight shows that as a teenager, I was no less troubled by the destruction of war than I was in my childhood, when I asked my father about the fires of World War II, or in my early youth, when I became obsessed with the prison camps of North Korea.

> Man that nobody dares to look at
> Sitting on the curb, ashamed,
> With one leg resting on the hard, cold cement,
> The other resting on a battlefield somewhere, rotting. . . .

Another of my characters outside the social mainstream was this black man, described in a spoken, vernacular language that I found in Sandburg and Williams:

> He told us stories and winked and
> laughed teeth across his wrinkly
> black face when we wanted to hear another one.

Narrated by a young speaker my own age, the poem concludes with the following twist:

> I used to like him when I was little,
> but then Pa told me to stay away from that place.

As I reread those lines about "Pa," the benighted father who passes racism on to his son, I recall the distrust I felt at seventeen toward fathers, and I think about the sympathy toward blacks I learned as a child from my mother.

Oddly enough, my stepfather, who had no interest whatever in my creative work, influenced it even more than my mother did. Because he moved the family to his acreage on the Connecticut River, I became acquainted with the rural life of northern New England, and this experience ultimately led me to a poetry of place.

In the book I wrote as a teenager there are no entries about my stepfather's small farm in West Claremont. That poetry would come later. There are, however, two poems about the Kuhre farm in the nearby township of Cornish, where he took me for a summer job when I was fifteen. I had been selected by my high school teachers that spring for a special summer program at Saint Paul's School in Concord, the state capitol, but as the fee for attending was $200, a large expense for my parents, my stepfather decided to sign me up for work on the Cornish dairy farm instead. I was not at all happy about the arrangement. Yet my experience at the Kuhre farm became so important to my understanding of New England that I returned to it often in my later writing.

No reader of my manuscript would guess I was thinking of that farm when I wrote these opening stanzas for a poem personifying time:

Time you
peaceful quiet lull of the virgin countryside
that we try to pierce stomp kill with concrete and car horns

Time you
careful beautiful building schizophrenic who is
ruthlessly raping wrecking ripping down . . .

I borrowed the approach of this rant about the evils of urban devel-
opment from passages in John Don Passos's U.S.A. trilogy and from
poems about the threat of mass society in Lawrence Ferlinghetti's *A Coney
Island of the Mind*. But the "virgin countryside" that inspired my fear of
the developers was the vast and beautiful expanse of hayfield, pasture-
land, and forest, which I first saw on the Kuhre farm in my fifteenth year.
By the time I wrote my poem about time, that farm represented in my
mind all the farmland that was falling into the hands of realtors during
the 1950s along the Connecticut River north of Claremont.

The attachment I felt to the Kuhre farm did not happen all at once.
I resented being volunteered there by my stepfather, and the dawn to
dusk schedule of milking cows, putting up silage, and gathering hay was
oppressive to me. Besides, I didn't take to the arrogant and uncommuni-
cative owner of the farm, Ludwig Kuhre. He was well into his seventies
at the time I arrived, a stroke victim who had lost one eye years before
when, in an accident of timing, one of his cows jerked its horns up as
he was leaning down to feed it grain. His right hand bore a scar from an
accident with a bandsaw. Each morning after breakfast, as Kuhre walked,
twisting himself step by step on his crutch out to his old tractor, one of
the first the John Deere company ever made, I turned its immense and
heavy flywheel to start it for him. Reaching the tractor, he would hoist
himself up into the seat—assistance was out of the question—hook his
crutch onto the gear shift, and head off to cut the hay with thunderous
chugs that shook the ground. At night after the milking when I sat down
to supper with him and his wife, she read aloud in Danish from an old
prayer book. Then the three of us ate leftovers from the noon meal as she
talked to him in their native tongue with scarcely a pause. Kuhre seldom
responded, only grunted and went on eating, the eyeless side of his face
turned toward me in the room's dim light so he seemed shut away from

me, too. In the daytime, when I looked up from my raking to find him cutting hay in a distant field with that eyeless profile, he seemed even more unreachable, closed away in the rituals of the Old World he went on imposing upon the land in Cornish, despite his disabilities.

On the day my stepfather drove me to meet the old man, I also met his son Andrew. Mrs. Kuhre was especially fond of Andrew. Though there was never any physical contact between the two of them, I could hear the tenderness she felt toward him in the way she spoke his name, "Ahnd-ruh," lingering over the first syllable and the "r." Andrew lived with his wife Vera and their young son in the upstairs apartment of the huge Kuhre homestead. He was a big, kindly man, more approachable by far than his father even though he shared Ludwig's taciturn manner. It was Andrew I often worked with during the summer of 1957, gradually bonding with him. I told him about saving the ten dollars I earned each week for an electric guitar and amplifier, and about my hope of starting a rock 'n' roll band. I also showed him the flat piece of wood I kept in my back pocket. On it I had drawn frets and stretched six strings so I could practice chords in my spare time.

Andrew reciprocated with bits of family history. I learned of his parents' arranged marriage that took place after Ludwig wrote back to Denmark for a wife, and of his younger brother's drowning in the farm's pond. Andrew also told me about neighboring dairy farms that had been sold off for development, and confided wistfully that his father's farm, the largest in Cornish and once the most prosperous, was now, after years of falling milk prices, little more than a break-even operation, all work and no profit. But his most worrisome confidence came during my school vacation in February, when I returned to the farm and help out with chores.

By then I was an old hand, trusted with all the work I was asked to do—helping to buck up firewood, shoveling out and liming stalls in the barn, and at milking time, putting the teat cups of the milking machine on the cows. These were things I was proud to know, particularly because I was not a mechanical person, often out of my element in my stepfather's self-made world that depended on practical skills. I was especially proud to be trusted with the secret Andrew shared with me that February, disturbing as it was. He had a hernia, he said, and he wasn't supposed to do any heavy lifting. "The doctor even says I should get out of the farming business," Andrew said.

"Couldn't you get an operation for it?" I asked him.

"Yup, I could" he said, turning his head back to the cow he was stripping in the tie-up. "But it would cost money, and then I'd be laid up for weeks with nobody to do my chores." He hadn't told his father yet, he added, and he didn't have to explain why. Leaving the farming business, as the doctor recommended, might have had its benefits for Andrew, but for Ludwig Kuhre, who had all along hoped to pass the farm on to his son, it would be devastating.

Andrew muddled on without an operation after I left him that February. But the demise of the farm came anyway. One summer afternoon Kuhre climbed down from his tractor in the field, perhaps to remove an obstacle, and forgot to put the brake on. As he bent over, the tractor rolled forward, knocking him down and killing him. It no longer seemed important to continue the farm work after that.

* * *

It would be years before I could find a way to tell the story of the Kuhre farm in poetry. But during my school vacation of 1959, I did the best I could. My head full of the mythological poems of T. S. Eliot that John Huot had sent me, I had an idea, which I shared with Andrew in the tie-up. I would write a poem that centered on the cows around us, locked in their stanchions. Bound as they were, they would symbolize the modern situation of the twentieth century, I told him. I would describe the whitewash of the barn walls in a way that suggested a hospital, a place of sickness. As for those who tended the cows in my poem, like him and me, I said, they would in a way be bound, too, waiting for spring to come and with it a change, perhaps a spiritual rebirth.

I still wince when I return to this memory of me as a kid so excited by the prospect of writing a poem, crazy as the poem was, that I discussed my plans for it at milking time with a literal-minded farmer who had no experience whatever with poetry. I wince again when I think of Andrew looking up from his milking stool to stare at me as if he were observing the slow growth of my second head.

In a different sense than I had in mind, of course, Andrew was bound to the farm. I see now that as a man in his middle thirties and a member of a generation with priorities far different from those of Ludwig Kuhre, Andrew was also bound to change, whether it disrupted the farm or not. When I first went upstairs in the Kuhre farmhouse to the apartment where Andrew and Vera lived, I was surprised by the contrast between it and the apartment I had left behind. Downstairs, where I had a room, was a closed system of prayer book readings in Danish, early bedtime (except for me, playing Fats Domino, Little Richard, and Buddy Holly down low on my portable radio), and a kitchen woodstove that turned out meals on the clock in the summertime for the family and the hired help. Upstairs, by contrast, there were plastic toys strewn from the son's bedroom to the living room, a TV that stayed on till late at night, and during the off-hours, regular guests from town. It was no wonder that Andrew spoke of the hardship of farm work and how little money he made from it. He was not from the Old Country after all, but from America, and in the 1950s, even as he carried out the rituals of farm labor inherited from his father, he had heard the call of another life.

In the end Andrew was not so different from my parents—my father, for instance, roughly Andrew's age, who felt the pull of a world beyond his father's farm, and my mother, who left her family's farm in her mid-teens, both of them trusting their fate to an America that was increasingly mobile and urbanized.

My stepfather, Paul Joly, belonged to a changing America no less than the others. For though he became a farmer as an adult, his farm was marked by the entrepreneurism of the 1950s, its thirteen acres used for a bootstrap operation of building a ranch-style house and starting a farm and nursery business while he worked at a machine shop. Like my mother and father, he left behind what seemed to him a closed system—in his case, a patriarchal French-Canadian family and a church that opposed his marriage—to improvise an identity for himself.

The elegies I finally wrote about the loss of the old agrarianism in New England came directly from my experience as a teenager on the Kuhre farm. In other poems, I wrote about the region that came next, my New England—a place of farmers under threat, ethnic shop workers, traders, and misfits at the margins—exploring their American dreams, failures, self-doubts, and restlessness. I got my first glimpse of that New England in the persons of Andrew Kuhre and Paul Joly.

Chapter 5

Fathers

Again it is the moment before I left home
for good, and my mother is sitting quietly
in the back seat while my stepfather pulls me
and my suitcase out of the car and begins
hurling my clothes . . .

—"After My Stepfather's Death"

I never intended to leave home when I got into my parents' car two
days after graduating from high school in June 1959. My only purpose
was to go to Claremont and take the test for my driver's license, which
I had prepared for by taking a course in driver education. Getting my
license was important because I had been hired as a driver and gardener
at the Ben Mere Inn in Sunapee, New Hampshire. My job at the Ben Mere
was to pick up guests in the company station wagon and take care of the
gardens. Yet for days my mother had refused to let me use the car for my
driver's test. Since I'd returned home after running away, she told me, she
hadn't liked my attitude one damn bit, and there was no way in hell she
was going to reward me by taking me to Claremont.

Now, on the very afternoon when I was supposed to show up at
the Ben Mere, my parents suddenly changed their minds. They would
drive me to take the test, my mother said, though only because they had
errands to do. "If you want a ride to Sunapee once the test is over," she
added, "you can just wait until we're done."

As I put my battered suitcase into the trunk my stepfather held open,
I wasn't concerned about being dropped off in Sunapee, but about our
late start. It was nearly four o'clock, and the town office closed at 4:30.

"We'll be lucky if the office is still open when we get there," I mumbled as we headed down the road. That remark ignited one last, unforgettable display of Paul's anger. Swerving to the side of the road, he slammed on the brakes, jumped out of the car, and flung open the back door. "Get the hell out of there," he said, yanking me out of my seat and reaching into the trunk for my suitcase, whose contents he spilled out onto the road. Then he pitched out my guitar case and my small amplifier, scooped up the clothes from the unlatched suitcase, and threw them into the air. "There, you goddamned little shit, you," he said and drove off toward Claremont without me, tearing through the gears.

Stunned, I watched until my parents were out of sight, hoping Paul might cool off and come back. But he didn't, and as the road fell silent, my own anger set in. I was now determined to leave West Claremont and never come back. I carried my luggage in two trips to the house, pried open the cellar screen, and went upstairs to get the rest of my things: the last books of the cache John Huot had sent to me and an unpressed white dress shirt I had picked out at a rummage sale and never worn because it required cufflinks. My hands shaking, I flipped through the yellow pages of the phone book and called a cab.

How much a cab ride might cost from West Claremont to Sunapee, a distance of thirty miles, I had no idea, but I began to suspect it would be more than the three dollars in my pocket, all the money I had. By the time the cab arrived, I almost expected to be turned down.

"I need to go to Sunapee," I said, "but all I have is three bucks." The cab driver, a tough-looking young woman who had no doubt experienced her own troubles with parents, assessed me from the window as I stood there beside my guitar, my amplifier and the scratched-up suitcase with an old dress shirt draped over it.

"Let's load your stuff into the trunk," she said.

As she drove toward Sunapee with one hand on the wheel and the edges of a tattoo showing under the short sleeve of her jersey, I told her about being thrown out of the family car, and how I picked up my clothes from the field and carried my stuff back to the house so I could use the phone. "This is the last time I'll ever go anywhere near that place," I told her.

When we unloaded my cargo at the Ben Mere, I held out my three dollars, but she brushed me aside and got back inside her cab. "You're going to need that," she said. "Good luck to you." Waving her tattooed arm, she drove away.

That generous act from a complete stranger altered my mood, making me see the possibilities of my situation. If she had helped me in this way, surely I could find a co-worker at the Inn with a car who would take me to Claremont or even Newport, closer by, for my driver's test. Maybe I could manage to get my license even before the season got going, and Mr. Burns, the burly, cigar-smoking manager who had hired me, would be none the wiser. I felt better still when Burns's assistant showed me my room. It had a desk where I could write poems in my time off, and a spare chair where I could practice my guitar.

In the morning the assistant put me to work weeding one of the gardens, and as I knelt among the flowers, I heard someone calling my last name. There in the driveway wearing his perennial brown suit and hat stood Mr. Burns, shaking a set of keys. "Forget the garden for now and drive me to Newport," he said. "I've got to go to the bank."

From the moment I sat behind the wheel of the station wagon, our trip was a disaster. I stared at the letters on the dash: P, R, D1, D2. The only cars I knew had manual shifts, and the wagon, an automatic, was a complete mystery to me. What did P, the gear the car was now in, stand for, and could you turn the engine over when the car was in P?

"Let's go. Start it up," Burns said, pulling a cigar out of his shirt pocket.

When I turned the key, the engine kicked in with no further event. Relieved, I looked at the letters again. R clearly meant reverse, but I couldn't decide which of the other gears to choose.

Burns was aghast. "Don't you know how to drive?" he asked.

"I've never tried an automatic," I answered. "But I'm guessing I should put it in D1."

"Yes, for Christ's sake, yes," Burns said, putting the cigar in his mouth. "Put it in drive."

I thunked the gear shift down to D1, and we lurched out of the driveway into town. Stopping quickly behind a car that turned into a side-street, I pressed my foot by habit on the nonexistent clutch and screeched the brakes.

"Oh, my God," Burns said, the cigar in his mouth still unlit.

When we reached the main road and headed toward Newport, I picked up speed. Should I stay in drive, I wondered, or shift to D2? If I didn't exceed 40 or 45 miles per hour, I told myself, I could placate Burns without ever having to find out.

We went a mile or so before Burns balked. "Can't you drive any faster than this? Jesus, I'd like to get there today, not tomorrow."

I shifted into D2, and the car broke into a roar.

"What are you doing?" he shouted. "Put it back in drive!" I rushed to do as he asked, reached once more for the clutch pedal, and hit the brakes.

"This is unbelievable," Burns said, returning his unlit cigar to his pocket.

But neither he nor I had seen the worst of it. When at last I pulled into a parking space on Newport's main street and he went into the bank, I decided to turn the car around so it was headed toward Sunapee before he could witness my lack of expertise with reverse gear. Somehow I put the car in drive rather than reverse, and it lunged forward, breaking a parking meter off at the base.

Before I knew it, there were people all around me—passersby, the hardware clerk, Mr. Burns, and a police officer, who ordered me out of the car and asked for my driver's license.

"I forgot it at the Inn," I lied.

The officer wrote down my name and home address. Then he tore off a ticket. "I want to see you at the station tomorrow morning," he said. "And bring that license."

As Mr. Burns drove us back to Sunapee, speeding much of the way, he had only one thing to say to me, more familiar than he knew: "What a hammerhead."

The following day I went to Burns's office and told him the story of why I didn't have a license, certain this would be the end of my career at the Ben Mere Inn. But Burns surprised me, first by clearing things up with the Newport police, then by sending me to his partner, Mr. Bodenstab, who ran the kitchen and had a job for a dishwasher. I spent the next several weeks trying to prove I wasn't a hammerhead after all, scrubbing the pots and pans until they shone, and bleaching all the grease out of the old floors. Yet I couldn't wash away the loneliness and rejection I had felt as I stood with my discarded belongings by the side of the road in West

Claremont. I went whole days without sleep. It hardly helped that when my brother John visited me at the end of the summer, he reported that my mother and stepfather had disowned me. "They say you broke into the house and stole things," he said.

* * *

My anxiety and insomnia continued throughout the fall at Keene Teachers College, where I entered the education program as an English major. I was at one and the same time elated to be living on my own, and plagued by a feeling of homelessness. That feeling went away only after I made friends with a couple of upperclassmen who had artistic inclinations like me, found a drummer and fellow guitarist to perform with at school dances, and got a girlfriend. Gradually, I began falling asleep everywhere. "Jesus, McNair," one of my friends complained when I fell asleep in his room. "You're drooling all over my roommate's bedspread." At the local beer joint that took my height of six-three as an indication I was old enough to drink, my girlfriend shook my arm to wake me. "For God's sake, Wes, open your eyes and finish your beer." Frustrating as my behavior was for all of them, it marked the beginning of my return to mental health.

Poetry also contributed to my restoration. On the first exam I took in college, a test on Beowulf and Chaucer for Malcolm Keddy's English Literature Survey, I scored a 96, beating out a junior girl who was known to be Keddy's best student. When we got to the poetry unit in freshman composition, which I also took with Keddy, I was the only student who spoke during discussions. A laconic Scotsman who seldom gave compliments, Keddy praised me after class. He didn't guess I had been coached in my comments on Cummings and Frost by R. P. Blackmur and Randall Jarrell, through volumes given to me by John Huot.

From Blackmur and Jarrell I learned that T. S. Eliot was widely seen as the most important poet of the period. By the time I was a junior at KTC and studied his work in Keddy's modern poetry course, Eliot was at the height of his renown, a recipient of the Nobel Prize in Literature. I discovered critics had based whole careers on explaining obscure references to mythology and English Literature in Eliot's work. Their essays about "The Waste Land," "The Hollow Men," and "Gerontian" fascinated me, as did Eliot's views of poetry in "Tradition and the Individual Talent."

Yet I was reading him not only as an English major but also as a writer in formation seeking something of use, and as a poet, I felt hemmed in by Eliot. How could I take his advice and "depersonalize" myself in the service of literary tradition without writing poems like his? I had already done that in high school. Now that I wanted to write poems of my own, I couldn't get Eliot out of my ear.

In the midst of my dilemma I found a small, white-covered volume in the KTC library by Karl Shapiro, titled *In Defense of Ignorance*, and it changed everything. I took the book home to my apartment and read most of its essays in a single night. Their call to arms against Eliot and the literary modernists spoke directly to the rebel in me, the twenty year old who had twice run away from home. As I read, I sensed that Eliot was not only Shapiro's literary father but also my own, and I wanted to join forces in bringing the elder poet down, together with his "dictatorship of intellectual modernism." I was particularly inspired by Shapiro's intention to reinstate "the right to create as he will to the poet." In my mind, I was that poet.

One afternoon at the University of New Hampshire I found another son who was rebelling against Eliot. Walking down the hall of the English Department, I heard fragments of a speech being delivered in an English classroom, and going to the door, saw that the speaker was a young, beardless W. D. Snodgrass, who had just won the Pulitzer Prize for his poetry collection, *Heart's Needle*.

I took a seat at the back of the room and listened as Snodgrass attacked the obscurantism of T. S. Eliot. American poetry needed a new model, he declared—not Eliot's French symbolists, but Geoffrey Chaucer. To the pleasure of his audience, he concluded the lecture by quoting from *The Canterbury Tales* and comparing Chaucer's earthiness and accessibility to the ethereal and abstract language of Laforgue and Mallarmé. I left the hall more determined than ever to seek a different way for my poetry.

As a junior at KTC, I rebelled not only against T. S. Eliot, but against the college itself. I had chosen to enroll there because I wanted to learn more about literature, my passion, and teach it to others. But after two years, I felt isolated by my intellectual inclinations. My upperclass friends had now graduated, and my girlfriend, a senior when I met her, had a job teaching school. I longed for classmates who might share my interests— also for professors who were less programmatic in their approaches and more curious about ideas. Where were the teachers who could help me with my poems? A girl I knew offered to show them to her professor. She was taking his course in recent literature, and she believed he was a published author. I carefully assembled a group of my poems, passed them on, and never saw them again.

Did I concentrate too much on the shortcomings of the students around me? Whether or not, I couldn't help cringing when a co-ed I knew asked if she could borrow my Thesaurus, which she called "Roger's Pocket Treasures." Once the professor of my English Literature class asked what Shelley meant when he wrote in his apostrophe to the skylark, "Bird thou never wert." A student answered that maybe the skylark had "never worked." Dating my girlfriend in Dover on weekends, I often visited the University of New Hampshire, which seemed a much livelier and more engaged campus. But the tuition there was more than I could afford. Returning each Monday to the more limited college I had chosen took me back to the feelings of failure and unworthiness I had felt in the dark days of West Claremont.

My mood shifted when I read an article called "Have Our Teachers Colleges Failed?" published in November by Evan Hill in *The Saturday Evening Post*. Hill's article was a diatribe against teacher education, and since he came from New Hampshire—from my birthplace of Newport, in fact—there was little doubt that Keene Teachers College and its sister college in Plymouth were primary targets. Teachers colleges, he wrote, were more concerned with teaching methods than with the quality of an intellectual experience. Mixing satire with reportage, he created a representative faculty member named "Professor Rosebud," an insipid figure who had no interest in thought and gave lectures from yellowed notes.

Hill's *Post* article did not go unnoticed at KTC. Shortly after it appeared, the president of the college, Lloyd P. Young, who scarcely ever stepped outside the ivy-covered walls of his official residence, invited Evan Hill to campus. His aim was to show the upstart reporter how misinformed he was about teachers colleges. Hill visited, but the lesson did not take. After spending a day at Keene Teachers College, Hill told the reporter from the *Keene Evening Sentinel* who accompanied him that he had seen nothing which changed his mind.

In its next issue the college newspaper, *The Monadnock*, ran a feature editorial in large print on its front page by President Young. Young scorned Hill as a critic who came to KTC with preconceived ideas. Teachers colleges, he asserted, boast a list of accomplishments that was easily "as long and impressive as Mr. Hill's list of weaknesses." A student letter on the opinion page also criticized Hill's article, though it was so muddled in its thinking it seemed only to prove Hill's point about the inferior education of KTC and its sister colleges.

The self-satisfaction and denial of the attacks on Evan Hill were all I needed to spring into action. I bought up every remaindered copy of Hill's *Post* article I could find in the city of Keene. Then I went to the florist shop to purchase roses—not rosebuds, which turned out to be too expensive, but disintegrating roses the florist was about to throw away, which conveyed their own message. I tucked one of these roses into each copy of my magazines and stole into the faculty mailroom, picking out the boxes of teachers who, in my view, most closely resembled Professor Rosebud. As I rolled up the magazines around their cargo and inserted them, I felt the thrill of insurrection. I saved the rottenest rose for the mailbox of Lloyd P. Young, the remote and scornful father of Keene Teachers College.

Evan Hill's article not only inspired my prank, it showed me how to express my disillusionment with KTC as a writer. Putting my poetry aside for the time being, I founded an underground newspaper which I called *Jabberwocky*, after the nonsense rhyme by Lewis Carroll, and began addressing the limitations I saw in KTC through a combination of commentary and satire. My newspaper's sole contributor, I wrote articles about the college's classes, fraternities, and student publications. I drew satiric cartoons as well, some of them single panels that featured campus characters, others in a comic-strip format resembling the strips of Jules Feiffer, which I loved. Somehow I prevailed upon the publisher of the *Keene Shopper*, a weekly advertiser, to run off the mimeographed pages of *Jabberwocky* at no cost. Working on each issue from start to finish, I was no longer so depressed about being at Keene Teachers College. As the year went on, I included reviews of foreign films seen in Boston, and wrote satires of New Hampshire's right-wing daily, *The Manchester Union Leader*, and the then ubiquitous American magazine, *TV Guide*.

Like Evan Hill, I was castigated by *The Monadnock*. An unnamed someone wrote a column mocking *Jabberwocky* and renaming me "I. J. Pulitzer McDragg." The associate editor sneered that I seemed to think KTC "is in even worse shape than the colleges depicted by Evan Hill in *The Saturday Evening Post*." He concluded: "If certain individuals on campus would spend less time criticizing and ridiculing those who are working, and spend more time working themselves, things would be better all around." Eventually, however, *Jabberwocky* helped me to find my own small community. A few students congratulated me, as did faculty members like Sprague Drennan, the reticent and gentlemanly chair of the English Department, whose taste for rebellious critique I would never have suspected. Malcolm Keddy joined in. When two students offended by a satire I had written about their fraternity printed a witless reply to *Jabberwocky* called *Jabbemouth* (sic), Keddy suggested ways of countering their publication in my next issue.

The best outcome, however, was my meeting with Roman Zorn, who had just been hired as dean of the college. When Zorn sent word that he wanted to see me about my newspaper, I expected the worst—expulsion or at least the threat of it. But as I entered his office, Dean Zorn stepped from behind his desk and shook my hand warmly and vigorously. An alternative newspaper like mine, he declared, was the sign of an intellectual life on campus. "I want to thank you for stirring things up here," he said. "That's what colleges are for."

Two years later Zorn replaced the paternalistic Lloyd P. Young as president. As a further indication of the college's increasing sophistication, KTC took on a new name, more in keeping with its expanding curriculum in the professions and the liberal arts: Keene State College. I see now that by assailing Keene's anti-intellectualism and provinciality in my alternative newspaper, I had engaged in a struggle that was larger than I thought.

I still remember the sunny morning in late spring when I returned to my apartment from Dean Zorn's office. As I walked in and out of the shadows of maple leaves dappling the sidewalk, I recited a John Keats sonnet I had recently memorized, "On First Looking into Chapman's

Homer." That sonnet about the power of the written word, in which Keats discovers a new translation of Homer and the glories of a great poet at the same time, fit my mood after hearing Zorn's praise of my own written words. The concluding lines of Keats's poem, likening his discovery of Chapman's Homer to the sighting of the New World, speak of silence, but I in my elation I delivered them full-voice, loud enough for the whole neighborhood to hear:

> Then felt I like some watcher of the skies
>   When a new planet swims into his ken;
> Or like stout Cortez when with eagle eyes
>   He star'd at the Pacific—and all his men
> Look'd at each other with a wild surmise—
>   Silent, upon a peak in Darien.

Chapter 6

The Future

... It's not easy to escape the past,
but who wouldn't want to live in a future
where the worst has already happened
and Americans can finally relax after daring
to demand a different way? For the rest of us,
the future, barring variations, turns out
to be not so different from the present
where we have always lived — the same
struggle of wishes and losses, and hope,
that old lieutenant, picking us up
every so often to dust us off and adjust
our helmets ...

—"The Future" (1)

I have a nasty note from Allen Tate to thank for the temporary peace I made with T. S. Eliot in the spring of 1962. Buoyed by the success of my satirical newspaper *Jabberwocky*, I developed the grand plan of a magazine featuring art and ideas. The problem of how I would actually produce the magazine, I left for another day, drafting letters requesting contributions from Herbert Gold, Bertrand Russell, Truman Capote, Ella Fitzgerald, and the Agrarian poets Allen Tate and John Crowe Ransom. The only one who wrote back was Allen Tate. In green ink, he chastened me for exploiting established writers to launch my magazine. I was hurt by his note, mostly because he was right. As I came to realize my publication was a pipe dream, I grew proud that Tate had sent me a response in his own hand and mentioned it to Malcolm Keddy, my father figure on the faculty, omitting the pesky detail of why Tate had turned me down.

Keddy was impressed. "Tate used to teach in the master's program at Vanderbilt University, in Nashville, Tennessee," he said. "John Crowe Ransom taught at Vanderbilt, too. They were part of a group down there called the Fugitives. The Vanderbilt program is topnotch," he added. "You ought to think about applying next year."

Keddy's suggestion appealed to me. I had first learned about the work of Tate and Ransom in his modern poetry course, where I discovered that as New Critics, they were associated with T. S. Eliot. Yet in poetry they seemed to go their own way, writing poems that were inclusive in their approach, and in Ransom's case, poems that I loved. By studying in the program they influenced, I thought, I might be able to find my way past Eliot and gain the academic pedigree I hadn't found at KTC, becoming a college teacher with an M.A., like Keddy. A few days after he made his suggestion, going to Nashville had become my dream and my salvation.

In the meantime, I took a job as a dishwasher at the Howard Johnson's restaurant in Keene. Each night after I propped up my Oscar Williams anthology of American poetry on the dishwasher and started my shift, I read poems and fantasized about teaching them as a college professor with a Vanderbilt degree.

But one night a beautiful young woman walked into the kitchen with an order from the counter. I took in her auburn hair, her slow walk that made even a waitress uniform look sexy, and her curious blue eyes glancing my way as she backed out of the kitchen door.

"Who was that?" I asked the chef in a low voice.

"That's Diane," he said. "Relax, McNair, she's married."

"Married," I repeated. But hadn't the look she gave me at the door shown she was intrigued by me as much as I was by her?

"Yeah, she's already taken. Anyway, I thought you were taken yourself."

He was right—sort of. I had gotten engaged in the previous year, and for a time that engagement, together with Diane's marriage, enforced a distance between the two of us. Then she began to give me rides home after work, and our conversations before she left me off lasted longer and longer. I discovered that her marriage was nearly over. She had begun dating her husband when she was a sophomore in high school and he was a senior and captain of the baseball team. When he graduated and went into the service, they conducted their courtship by letter, her letters a good deal more frequent than his. After his return, much to the dismay of her parents, who had never liked him much, they got married, moving to an army base in Kansas City. Gradually she grew tired of his long absences, his continuous affairs, and his Johnny Cash music. She packed up their car and drove back to New Hampshire with their two children. Now she was suing for divorce.

I understood that Diane's confidence about her failed marriage, spoken between the two of us in the dark car, was partly an invitation, and it stirred my feelings for her. On the other hand, learning that she had two children scared me. Maybe we were better off remaining friends, I thought. When I told my fiancée Claire about the waitress who was driving me home after my shift, she wanted a description of her. "There's nothing to worry about," I assured her. "The two of us are just friends." Still, Claire pressed me to take her to the restaurant one Saturday when she was free from her job as an elementary school teacher. She wanted to be introduced to this woman named Diane.

If Claire intended to discourage the romance she feared, she ended by encouraging it. While she sat at the counter waiting to be introduced as the woman I was engaged to, I began to think about how to break the engagement off. Watching Diane take down the orders of other customers and reach up to the shelf for ice-cream cups with her long, graceful body and delicate hands, I wanted only her.

On the way back to my apartment, Claire and I fought about Diane, then made up. Over the next couple of weekends we fought some more, drifting toward our inevitable breakup. Meanwhile the conversations with Diane after work continued. I told her about my family in West Claremont, which by then I had begun to visit, missing my sister Karen. Diane had moved back in with her family in Keene, she said, taking the room where her father, a jazz musician and photographer, had stored musical equipment. Music, she told me, was one of her great loves. On summer nights when she was in high school, she sat on her porch listening to a neighbor's son, who later became a concert violinist, play concertos by Tchaikovsky and Mendelssohn. We decided we liked the Mendelssohn concerto best. We talked about favorite painters. She had painted watercolors, she said, and longed to paint again. My own dream, I replied, was to become a poet.

The next night, parking outside my apartment, she reached into the backseat for a book by Edna St. Vincent Millay and read "First Fig," a favorite of hers, aloud:

> My candle burns at both ends,
>   It will not last the night;
> But ah, my foes, and oh, my friends—
>   It gives a lovely light.

The poem was new to me. Committed to the canon of modernism, my teachers at KTC had never taught the poetry of Millay. But I was struck by its simple imagery and especially by its feeling, the more extravagant for Diane's slow reading. She read the poem again, this time accompanying it with "Second Fig":

> Safe upon the solid rock the ugly houses stand:
> Come and see my shining palace built upon the sand!

Then she looked at me. "What do you think?" she asked.

"Here's what I think," I said. I reached over, drew her close to me and kissed the mouth that had read the words. "I think I love you," I said.

"I was hoping you'd say that," she answered, "because I love you, too." She closed her eyes and kissed me back. Then she read more of her favorite poems and we kissed again. My head full of Millay's poetry and Diane's words of love, I sat up for hours after she left, stunned by the realization that I had at last found someone of my own kind.

Not long afterward, when we had graduated from conversations in the car to dates, Diane phoned to tell me she was taking her kids on a picnic for dinner.

"I'm driving them to the park," she said. "Want to come?"

I was waiting outside when she arrived at my apartment, and she pulled the children toward her on the bench seat to make room for me.

"This is David," she said pointing down at her older son with the carrot-top. "And this," she added, ruffling the brown hair of the other boy as he smiled and turned his face into her blouse, "is Bashful. No, I mean Joel."

They were very handsome little boys. They were also very active. At the picnic area of the park, Diane couldn't get them to stop running after each other and shrieking. And when she spread the blanket out and put our dinner on it, they ran right across the paper plates, upending the casserole. "Oh, no," she said. We shook the blanket off over the trash barrel and packed the kids back into the car. Full of apologies, she dropped me off hungry at my apartment.

The next week another dinner was upended. Diane and I stopped to pick up a pizza we had ordered at the local pizzeria, and as I turned from the cash register with our box in my hand, a muscular man rose from his table and hit me so hard in the face, he knocked me to the floor and the pizza flew halfway across the restaurant. I discovered later the man who threw the punch was Buzzy Houghton, a runner-up in the state Golden Gloves championship. Mentally challenged, Buzzy had been convinced by Diane's ex that I was a bad man who was breaking up their marriage and taking his kids away from him. As I gazed up from the floor stroking my jaw, I saw Diane thrash Buzzy with her pocketbook and scream at him while he backed away and tried to explain himself.

"I don't care what he told you, it's all lies. Now look what you did, you crazy jerk."

On the other hand, what had I done? Falling in love with Diane, I'd been taken deeper and deeper into problems that seemed too big for me to deal with. How, I asked myself, could I ease this woman out of a bitter marriage, join her ready-made family, and go to graduate school at Vanderbilt, too?

I decided I needed a break to think things over. Learning that the manager of the Keene Howard Johnson's was transferring to Beverly, Massachusetts, I asked him for work there and got a dishwashing job like the one I had, this time on the day shift. Diane seemed to take my departure in stride. She understood perfectly, she said. Was she so sanguine because she sensed I would be back?

It turned out that my coworkers in the kitchen at the Beverly Howard Johnson's, both older than I was, were evenly divided on the question of whether I should continue my relationship with a woman who had two children. The counter man, who had family difficulties and children of his own, was dead set against it. But the unmarried chef, suffering regrets about his breakup with a long-term girlfriend, said the point was how much I loved Diane. Meanwhile, I spent more and more of my spare time writing to her.

Diane would probably have liked more talk about love than she found in my letters. In one of them, I showed off my knowledge of Henry Miller's *Tropic of Cancer*, my favorite book at the time, writing Miller-like descriptions of the natural world I found in the coastal town of Beverly. In another, I urged her to listen to the music of Richard Strauss and sent her a *New York Times* review of Igor Stravinsky's dance-drama "The Flood," which she had seen on television. When I wrote about a beautiful sunset I wished she could share, I spent too much time on the sunset and not enough on my desire to be with her.

The balance was better in the passage I wrote later on about guitars. In it I likened both the acoustic guitar I had brought with me and the guitars of Cubist paintings to the loveliness of a woman's body, with Diane's body in mind. Overtired when I drafted my letter, I began with the salutation, "Dear Claire." Diane was not happy with my mistake. She fired back a letter pointing out the error. "Actually," she wrote, "I'm not Claire, I'm Diane." Stricken with guilt, I walked down the street to a pay phone and called her. "I'm not really upset," Diane told me. "I just miss you." We talked until all my coins were gone. Then I waited in the phone booth while she called me back to talk some more. By the time we hung up, I had promised to return as soon as I could.

In late July, when my old dishwashing job opened up at the Keene Howard Johnson's, I gave my notice in Beverly, packed up my few belongings, and hitchhiked to Keene. The joy I felt as I walked down the main street of the city in the sunshine with my satchel and guitar case resembled my elation three or four months earlier after my meeting with Dean Zorn. Then, I walked back to my apartment reciting John Keats's sonnet in full volume. On this day, though, I was whistling the main theme from Mendelssohn's Violin Concerto, which by then Diane and I had adopted as our love song. Suddenly, I heard a familiar voice calling my name, and as I turned, I saw Diane in her tank top and flip-flops, standing by a store front.

"Wesley?" she said.

We were both shocked to find each other there, and as the shock wore off, a little shy after all our time apart.

"That stuff looks awfully heavy," she said. "Would you like me to give you a ride?"

I loaded my things into her car, and she drove to the park where we'd had our unfortunate picnic weeks before. Then she turned off the ignition and slid over. We held each other and kissed for a long time.

"What are the chances of meeting up like that?" Diane asked, drawing back to look into my eyes. "Of you, coming down the street whistling the Mendelssohn concerto, and me hearing it, then walking out of the store to find you?" It was no coincidence, we decided. It had to be a sign of our new beginning. That afternoon at her parents' house, while the kids napped, we looked through the newspaper and found a room for me. The following weekend, free from work, we left the children with Diane's mother and drove to Boston, visiting the Museum of Fine Art for the first time and splurging on our first shared records: recent releases featuring Miles Davis and John Coltrane, the Ornette Coleman Quartet, and a new folk singer, Joan Baez. On the way home, we began to talk about marriage.

High on planning for our future, I began to see that getting a graduate degree from Vanderbilt once we got married was not only possible, but necessary. How else, I said to Diane, would I be able to get a college teaching position and support the family? A salary from a high school teaching job just wouldn't cut it. "We could all go down to Nashville together," I said. "All we'd need is some scholarship aid and a small loan from the bank." In my new optimism I also realized I had been making too much of my responsibilities as a father. Why couldn't we take periodic vacations from the children at the start of our marriage, I asked, going off somewhere to be with each other while they stayed with babysitters or her parents? Diane thought it was a good idea.

Gradually the children, who had once seemed an obstacle to our marriage, became a principal reason for it. I didn't want David and Joel to repeat the experience of my own fatherless childhood. Besides, I was pleased by how much my becoming a father meant to my mother. When I took Diane to West Claremont to meet her and Paul, my mother was ecstatic. She found in Diane, a divorced woman with children, an exact replica of herself years before in Southview. In her eyes, I was the hero who was rescuing an abandoned woman and single mother, just as my stepfather had once rescued her.

We got married in the Unitarian church on December 24, 1962, I twenty-one and Diane barely twenty-two, our families and a few friends in attendance. Diane's mother couldn't believe our choice of date. "How are you ever going to keep your anniversary separate from Christmas?" she asked. There would just be one more reason to celebrate, we told her. It was harder to deal with the concerns of my brother John. He was then in his second year at Keene Teacher's College, having followed me there, and I chose him as my best man. As I drove him to the church in Diane's car on the day of the wedding, he pleaded with me not to marry her.

"I've been trying to stay out of this and keep my mouth shut," he said, "but when I got up this morning and started putting on my suit, I realized I had to say something. For Christ's sakes, Wes, if you marry this woman, you're going to be poor for the rest of your life. And you can kiss any thought of going to graduate school or being a poet goodbye. You'll be working your ass off just to support your family. It's not too late, you can stop this," he said.

"Have you gone nuts, Johnny?" I said, shocked and deeply offended. "We'll have problems, sure. But everybody does. Besides, I love this woman you're talking about."

During the ceremony, Diane on one side of me in a beautiful teal blue dress, Johnny on the other, I tried to get his words out of my mind. I was relieved that Johnny handed me my ring without event, and that he said nothing when the minister called on those who objected to our marriage to speak now or forever hold their peace. Then the minister pronounced us man and wife. I turned to take Diane into my arms and for the moment forgot everything but our kiss.

It didn't take long for the hardships my brother predicted to engulf us. After paying for the wedding party at my in-laws' house, we drove to New York City for a weekend honeymoon, returning to discover that the manager of the Howard Johnson's, under the impression I would not be returning to the restaurant after our marriage, had replaced me with another dishwasher. Two weeks later, when my replacement didn't work out and I was rehired, Diane and I were flat broke, lacking even the ten dollars we owed the church organist who played at our wedding. Instead of taking vacations away from the kids in my final college semester as we had planned, we worked longer hours than ever to make ends meet, choosing opposite shifts whenever we could to avoid hiring babysitters.

While Diane waitressed, I combined study and childcare at the married couples' barracks where we lived. But studying proved hard to do. David and Joel were often as wild as they had seemed when I first met them, screeching through the apartment and fighting over toys. The punishment I favored as their new father was to make each sit quietly in a chair, though they quickly grew restless and fidgety. It would be years before I learned why. They had what later came to be known as ADHD, attention deficit hyperactivity disorder. Being still was what they were least able to do.

Never mind, I told myself when my brother John's warnings came to mind. I always had my application to Vanderbilt. One cold night in January, when Diane and the kids were in bed, I sat close to the space heater in our primitive apartment and wrote the centerpiece of my application, an essay about why I wanted to enroll in the English program. If I had been smart, I would have emphasized the poetry and criticism of Allen Tate and John Crowe Ransom in my essay. Instead, I held up D. H. Lawrence as my literary model, writing and revising with great excitement until dawn. I had loved Lawrence's poetry ever since I read Karl Shapiro's praise of it in *In Defense of Ignorance*. Lawrence, Shapiro said, offered an alternative to the work of the literary modernists. It did not occur to me that the literary modernists included Ransom and Tate.

But somehow I got in. One day during April when I returned from an errand in town with David, who liked to sit in my lap in the pre-seat-belt period holding the steering wheel as I drove, Diane came out into the yard of the barracks with Joel, waving a stamped envelope from Vanderbilt. "I just know you've been accepted," she said, and she was right. I read the letter aloud to her, and we hugged each other and shouted and hugged again. "We did it!" I shouted, including in my triumph all four of us, my new family. I was sure my success resulted from the essay I wrote about poetry. Through it, I had struck a blow against doubt—my brother's and my own—and restored my future as a teacher and a poet.

* * *

Yet how could I get to that future without paying the bills that had already built up and putting some money ahead? There was no way except to defer the acceptance at Vanderbilt and teach high school for a year. I didn't mind. If I had no money, I at least had my acceptance. And I warmed to the idea of trying my hand at teaching while supporting my new family with my first-time salary. I took a job as a teacher of the upper grades at a small high school in Hillsborough, New Hampshire, asking my mother to sew me two sport coats so I could switch them from week to week. Not far from the high school, in the town of Hancock, Diane and I found a cottage for rent with a combined living and dining area, two bedrooms, and a screen porch. It had its own private meadow and woods, and a campy feeling that we both loved. Before we even moved in, Diane got a job as a waitress at the Hancock Inn.

On Labor Day, as we unpacked boxes and the kids played in the yard, Diane looked out the kitchen window and began to scream. Joel had pulled himself up onto the rotting boards that lay across the dug well. I ran out to the well and swooped him off it. "Don't ever go near that again!" I shouted in a panic and brought him inside, where Diane lectured him some more. Before we could get the well cover replaced, there was another crisis. Our cat jumped onto the boards, fell through them and drowned. The whole family was upset, nobody more than me, since I had to retrieve the cat. Lowering a long ladder I found in the shed into the well, I thought of what might have happened to Joel on a less fortunate day. When the ladder touched bottom and I climbed stone by stone down into the dark listening to the sound of my breathing, I thought also of my stepfather going down into another well years before and being temporarily trapped there.

The incident at the well made me even more serious about my rules for the ever-active Joel and David. It was up to us, I told Diane, to "make them mind," using my mother's words. Anyway, I had taken a college course in psychology that showed patterns of behavior were formed at an early age. Now was the time we should be teaching David and Joel how to focus all this energy of theirs, I said. And how could they learn respect for us as parents if we didn't insist on a few things, like not talking back, and cleaning up their plates at mealtimes? "When I was a kid," I reasoned, "I didn't always like the food I was served, either, but eating it helped me to form good eating habits." We needed to make the kids sit at the table until they ate what was on their plates, I said, and when they needed a spanking, they should get one.

Grave as parenting became for me, it didn't allow for a lot of family fun. Diane and I worked so many hours, there wasn't much time for family fun anyway. After dinner with the kids, she left housework behind for her long night shift at the Inn. The parent on duty, I sometimes put the kids to bed by reading them a story or singing a song like "Froggy Went A-Courtin'" or "Fox Went Out on a Chilly Night," as I played my guitar. More often I skipped that part, turning as soon as I could to preparations for teaching the next day. Up the following morning at 6:30 a.m., I started in again, using weekends to correct the class papers that accumulated during the week.

I loved being a teacher. Finding ways to excite students about imaginative literature seemed to me the work I was born to do. Still, my teaching not only ate up family time but also threatened to consume me. Dressed in the two jackets my mother had handsewn, their thin lapels gradually curling upward, I taught back-to-back classes, supervised cafeteria duty, and talked to students individually during my free period. Though I set up the free period for class issues, what my students wanted to talk about was their personal troubles. On one afternoon a group of seniors came to me in grief because a classmate had shot himself to death. On another, a college-track girl confided that she and her sister had been molested by their father, a well-known figure in the town. Sometime later a girl and a boy who were going steady showed up, both frightened because she was going to have a child. *What can we tell our parents?* they wanted to know.

Meanwhile, I struggled for answers of my own. How could I control my teaching time so that it wasn't controlling me? How could I find more time to write? Why wasn't there ever enough money to go around, even though Diane and I both had jobs? And what had happened to the loving companionship she and I once knew during our beautiful courtship? Lonely for that love, I got an extension cord one spring night after the kids were in bed, carried our hi-fi to the front door of the cottage, and invited her to sit in the grass while we listened to the last movement of Mendelssohn's Violin Concerto.

For all the struggles of my year as a high school teacher in Hillsborough, I didn't want it to come to an end. I missed my students even as I taught them in my final weeks. I was so choked up when the seniors rose to give me a standing ovation at their year-end dinner, I could hardly manage to thank them. Shortly before their graduation, Diane gave me my first family birthday party at our house in Hancock. The kids were as anxious as she was for me to open my gifts and find the surprises inside. Basking in their affection, I wanted to stay right there in our first home and never leave it.

But by late June my family was already living in the duplex we had rented for the summer in Keene. Our dear meadow and woods were replaced by a large vacant lot, where cars from a tenement house parked, and no grass grew. During the day, I was a tender for a mason who built cement block houses; at night, Diane worked at still another waitress job. As I fed David and Joel the dinner she had prepared, I tried to ignore the domestic fights next door, which were continuous. After I'd put the kids to bed and the neighbors quieted down, I studied French for the language test scheduled that fall at Vanderbilt. Then I turned to my journal, writing descriptions of my coworkers for practice, and promising myself success in the long-term goal I had set for myself. "Whatever happens," I wrote, "I'm going to prevail."

Prevailing wasn't so easy. For one thing, we needed money. Saving for Nashville had proved hard to do, and even though Diane planned to work there, we wouldn't have enough to live on. Undeterred, I went to a local bank and applied for a loan, which the manager assured me I would get. When my summer boss suddenly lost a building contract and let me go, I checked the want ads and found a new job painting apartments downtown. There seemed to be no challenge I couldn't overcome until Diane walked through the door of an apartment I was painting in August, just weeks away from our flight to Nashville. "The doctor says I'm almost two months pregnant," she said, scarcely getting the words out before she began to weep. I climbed down from my stepladder and we sat together on the drop cloth for a long time, disconsolate about an event that would have made most young couples happy. "How am I going to get a job when I'm expecting?" Diane asked. It now seemed clear that we wouldn't be going to Nashville at all.

Yet when I got home, Diane had exchanged tears for conviction. "You're going to Vanderbilt," she said. "I've thought it all out. The kids and I will live with my grandmother for the year, in Goffstown."

"But who's going to support you while I'm gone?" I asked.

"I'll find some part-time work until the baby comes," Diane said. "I can take care of her, and she'll take care of me."

It all sounded workable. Her grandmother Bertha would, I knew, be thrilled to have her around. I was worried that I would miss the birth of our baby, but then I had a thought.

"If I'm traveling down there alone, we'll have money for me to fly back in April," I told her. So when late August came, I helped Diane move into Bertha's house. Then the two of us drove to Logan Airport in Boston for my night flight to Nashville.

Be careful, the expression goes, about what you wish for. Checking in at the travel counter in the airport, Diane by my side, the anticipation I had felt all summer turned to anxiety and dread. Why was I leaving, when all I really wanted to do was get back into the car with her and drive as far away from this place as I could get? As we held each other at the flight gate for one last kiss, we were both near tears. But Diane insisted on no second thoughts. "Walk right down that ramp, honey," she said, "and don't turn around." Then she was gone, and I was sitting on a plane for the first time in my life, heading toward Vanderbilt.

The day after I arrived in Nashville, I rented a room just off campus and set out to explore on foot the university I had chosen. I was shocked to find rows of frat houses and dormitories with competing rock music blasting from the windows. Wasn't Vanderbilt supposed to be a bastion of the contemplative life? Walking farther, I ran across a man on the grounds crew and asked for the location of the English Department. He pointed to a path that led through lawns and trees. "You're not far," he said, "just look for Old Central." Old Central turned out to be an unpretentious brick building with a small, pillared porch. I climbed the steps and found a wooden sign that took me by surprise. "Through these halls," it declared, "passed the Fugitives—1922-1925."

Those solemn words, taking me back to my first conversation about Vanderbilt with Malcolm Keddy, gave me comfort in the face of my apprehension and loneliness. I was standing in the very place where the Fugitives stood, this entryway now my own entry into the department where they once congregated. As I started my courses that week, some of them held in Old Central, I began to get my bearings. I especially liked my classes on Chaucer and the Romantic poets with Professor Duncan, the English Department chair. "Duncan can teach," I wrote to Diane. Yet when I went to the library to read my assigned essays by Hazlitt on the Romantic poets, I couldn't concentrate for missing her. The brave front I sensed in her regular letters from Goffstown only made things worse. How, I asked myself, could I have imagined spending months apart from her in this place of strange accents and live oaks with Spanish moss, holed up alone in a room? It gradually became clear to me that the home of the Fugitives would not be my home unless I could bring her and the children there.

Had we really done our best to find a family budget we could live on in Nashville? I made new calculations, mailing them off to Diane and asking her to see what was holding up the loan that could make our year together possible. Then I went on a search for apartments in Nashville with a realtor named John Lovelady, an upbeat man with cowboy boots and a comb-over, who insisted I call him Johnny. Despite Johnny's cheerfulness, my anticipation turned to despair. Everything he showed me exceeded the estimate I'd made for family housing. Our last stop was the cheapest two-bedroom rental on his list. The windows of its kitchen and living room had been smashed by the previous tenant. "We would of course replace the windows," Johnny Lovelady said.

It wouldn't have helped if he did. Sleazy as this rental was, it was still beyond the allowance in my new budget. Standing beside shards of broken glass, all that was left of my hopes, I began to sense I had underestimated other items as well. I returned to my room, lay on the bed for a long time, then decided to pack it in. Using most of my remaining money to purchase a bus ticket for Manchester, New Hampshire, and phoned Diane that I was coming home.

What happened to the loan the bank manager promised? Did he change his mind? Did the paperwork get stalled or lost? I never found out, and anyway the issue was moot. On my way back north, unwinding the journey I had made to Tennessee state by state, I rethought my dream for the future. The idea of getting a degree from Vanderbilt that would advance me professionally and lift my family's prospects at the same time had one crucial flaw: I had to leave the family to get it. In the process of going to Nashville, I had caused an anguish that would only grow as time went on. I hadn't bargained for the anguish. The only alternative I could

think of now was piecing together a graduate degree during summers—
a marathon that would take five years, while I taught in a public school.
What, in the meantime, was to become of my poetry?

Cruising into the terminal in Manchester after a trip of thirty-six
hours, I spotted Diane, beautiful as ever, waiting for me under the lights,
and I put aside my troubling thoughts. In fact, I could hardly believe my
luck. "I'm so glad you're back," Diane said as we embraced each other
beside the bus. "My God, it's been so long," I answered, though in fact
we'd been apart for less than a month.

In the sunshine of the next morning, David and Joel were each part
of the luck I felt. Everyone was happy at breakfast except Diane's grand-
mother, who seemed distant. After my self-examination on the bus, I
saw why. In her eyes I was a thoughtless husband who had left his preg-
nant wife and two children behind while he went off to pursue a college
degree hundreds of miles away. It was impossible to explain myself to
her because she never raised the subject, probably loving Diane too much
to make a scene. But on my second day in Goffstown, unnerved by her
suspicious expressions, I called up my mother. To her, I was still the hero
who had married a woman with two children. She would understand that
I went to Tennessee to help my family, even though my trip had not ended
well. "Until I find a job at a high school, I could earn my keep by doing
work around the nursery," I told her.

Which is how I ended up re-digging, in the fall of 1964, the long,
narrow trench I once dug from my parents' house to the riverbank,
the very trench featured in two photographs from my mother's album,
respectively titled "Digging" and "and Digging." The task this time was
to replace the septic pipe my stepfather had installed back then, now
badly damaged. My digging brought back the endless cycle of chores in
my childhood and youth, for I was not only up to my waist in a ditch but
also waist-deep in the work life of my parents. Their long days of labor
on the nursery, I came to see, were as joyless as the work days I had
spent growing up.

Nor did I escape blame for leaving my family behind for Tennessee.
One morning as I dug, my mother stood above me to give a speech she
had obviously prepared. "You've got to realize you have bills to pay and
a family to support just like everybody else," she said. "You can't just go

running off when you want to." Though she did not add "like your father," she might as well have. His abandonment was clearly on her mind.

I was outraged. "I will never become the kind of man who compromises his true life just to work and pay bills," I told her, taking a swipe as I made my point at what seemed to me the emptiness of her work ethic.

While I dug down through layers of riverbed clay toward the cracked PVC pipe that afternoon, I turned the words I had spoken over and over in my mind, finding solace in them. I was a person with a true life, I thought to myself, the life of a writer, and I would preserve that life. I began to see that even though I lost my dream of graduate school at Vanderbilt, I had made a new promise to the future. That promise helped me to ignore the ties I also felt to the past—my worries that I really had been a deserter, like my father, and that my journey had led me right back to my stepfather's farm, where I shoveled up the burbling pipe he had laid years before.

Chapter 7

The Briar Pipe

Married that young, with two children
and one more on the way, I lived far
from the still, beautiful place
where writers and scholars were photographed
in the early 1960s, so I studied each detail of it
on their dust jackets — the neat spines
of books arranged around them as they sat
contemplating something at the edge
of the picture frame in their sweaters
or tweeds, pipes in their hands. Buying a pipe
to hold in my hand, too, I couldn't quite
get over the taste of tar, and when I puffed it
in the calm, unhurried way I imagined,
it always went out . . .

               —"The Future" (2)

In the fall of 1964, my Plan A in ashes, I developed a Plan B, which
began with taking a position in a sixth-grade class in Newport, the only
job I could find. Then I turned my back on poetry. It was poetry that had
gotten me into this fix, after all. The poems by New Critics that drew me
to Vanderbilt suddenly seemed literary and false, irrelevant to the real-life
troubles I had begun to know as a married man with a family. I would try
my hand, I told Diane, as a fiction writer and a cartoonist.

    Looking back on my single-panel cartoons today, I see signs of my
disillusionment that autumn. One shows my impatience with art that
required special explanations. A woman stands in front of a blank canvas
at an exhibition gesturing to her companion. "He seems to have a way of

letting you know what he means," she remarks, "without really telling you." Another cartoon suggests the conflict I had started to feel about the duties of family. In it, a dejected cave man with a spear on his shoulder pauses at the opening of his cave, about to face his day. Beside him his wife, holding a newborn, says, "Maybe you should ask yourself whether it is making you grow as a person." There is more disillusionment in my cartoon about Superman, who sits at a bar with his drink wearing a slightly dazed expression. "Truth, justice and the American way seemed so right for awhile," he says, "and then I began to ask myself was I really happy."

As the fall went on, I was happy enough. Diane and I located an attractive cape-style house for rent outside of town, and I found that my position as an elementary school teacher had a special blessing. My preparations were less strenuous than they had been in Hillsborough, and the papers of my students were easier to correct. This allowed me more time off for my short stories as well as my cartoons.

In April, Diane gave birth to a son and I was happier still. Never mind that during the previous fall, I drew a newborn in the arms of my cave wife to express mixed feelings about family. Glimpsing our son for the first time through the window of the maternity ward delighted me, and when Diane held him and looked down at his face, she seemed to me more beautiful than ever. "He's the longest baby ever recorded at the Newport hospital," she said proudly. We named him Sean Jeffers, his first name for Sean O'Casey, the Irish playwright we both admired, his second for Robinson Jeffers, whose poetry we had discovered together.

When she got back home, her mother Sue arrived from Keene to help out, and our house was a joyful place of mothering and cooing. The first photographs Diane took of Sean show me lying on the rug next to him on his blanket, and lifting him above my head to surprise him into laughter. The pleasure and love in the snapshot are impossible to miss. Yet my elation had a flip side. It made me aware of a difference between my fatherly feeling for Sean, which was instant, and my feelings for David and Joel, which were burdened by a sense of responsibility. Wanting to show my stepsons the feeling my stepfather never showed me, I felt guilty about the two different loves. At night as they lay ready for sleep, I continued to sing folk songs on my guitar, and when friends visited, I invited them to help me improvise elaborate bedtime stories. But when our